REVENGE
OF THE
RICH

REVENGE OF THE RICH

THE NEOLIBERAL REVOLUTION IN BRITAIN AND NEW ZEALAND

AUSTIN MITCHELL

Biteback Publishing

First published in New Zealand by Canterbury University Press
This edition published in Great Britain in 2017 by
Biteback Publishing Ltd
Westminster Tower
3 Albert Embankment
London SE1 7SP

ISBN 978-1-78590-281-9

10 9 8 7 6 5 4 3 2 1

A CIP catalogue record for this book is available from the British Library.

Set in Adobe Caslon Pro

Printed and bound in Great Britain by
CPI Group (UK) Ltd, Croydon CR0 4YY

CONTENTS

FOREWORD

I READ THIS BOOK with great interest as it comments on events in my country and that of my forebears over the course of my lifetime.

Throughout the book, Austin Mitchell's passion for reducing inequality shines through. The welfare state created in post-war Britain by Clement Attlee and driven by key ministers like Nye Bevan was a serious attempt to address longstanding structural inequalities in society. In New Zealand, a leftish Liberal government in the 1890s and early 1900s had introduced old-age pensions, the vote for women, industrial conciliation and arbitration, and public housing. That thrust for inclusion and fairness was broadened and deepened by the Labour government of 1935–1949.

These initiatives meant that my generation of New Zealanders and Austin's generation of British citizens enjoyed more security and opportunity than previous generations ever had. Yet both countries eventually ran into difficulties over generating enough growth, revenue and work to meet the expectations of citizens.

In response, both reached for Friedmanite solutions, rather than emulating the more pragmatic approach of northern European economies. The Rhenish economic model, or social market economy, and the Nordic social democracy model have both been more successful in sustaining opportunity and security for populations than has neoliberalism.

In their different ways, the Blair/Brown governments in Britain and the Fifth Labour Government which I led in New Zealand endeavored to address the consequences of the neoliberal experiment. Both were big investors in public services like education and health.

In New Zealand we were bolder in tackling the neoliberal ideology of "less state, more market". We raised taxes, introduced a major cash transfer system – Working for Families, which demonstrably reduced income inequality – and increased the social wage in many other ways, including through more support for primary health care, early childhood education and child care, paid parental leave and longer annual holidays. We stopped state asset sales and bought back major transport assets like the national airline and the rail system, which had failed under earlier privatisation; made the State active again in economic strategy by designating enabling sectors and by boosting research and development spending and skills training to help lessen dependence on commodity trade; exited from private prison provision; created a sovereign wealth fund to back the universal pension and created a voluntary savings scheme to complement the basic provision – and much else besides. Net Crown debt was zero at the time the global financial crisis hit in 2008, which gave New Zealand considerable fiscal space to respond to it.

The political cycles which brought Labour to power in both countries ended, and conservative governments returned. In New Zealand, however, the advent of proportional representation in 1996 served to stop extreme lurches in policy. While a number of policy changes have occurred, as one would expect with a change in government, much of the legacy of the 1999–2008 Fifth Labour Government remains intact.

Both countries, however, face higher inequalities than they had in the immediate post-war years. Austin refers in the book to "the left-behind people". The rapid structural adjustments in a number of Western economies have resulted in many such people. Some don't vote at all. Others lash out at those they hold responsible for their circumstances. We live in polarised and polarising times.

I look for hope in the new global agenda signed on to by all nations – the 2030 Agenda for Sustainable Development. Its fundamental premise is to "leave no one behind". That is as relevant to New Zealand and Britain today as it is to any developing country. If our countries and our world continue to accept inequalities and exclusion on today's scale, then we will continue to reap what that sows – division, envy and even hatred. That is not a recipe for harmonious societies, nor for a harmonious world.

Agree with it or disagree with it, love it or loathe it, Austin Mitchell's writing provokes us to reflect on what our common future could be. It is written in a lively fashion with highly quotable turns of phrase. I commend it to all readers.

Rt Hon. Helen Clark
Former Prime Minister of New Zealand 1999–2008

PREFACE

NEOLIBERAL ECONOMICS HAVE DOMINATED economic policy in Britain, New Zealand and much of the advanced world for the last four decades. Introduced in Britain by Margaret Thatcher, and in New Zealand by Roger Douglas, the ideology has travelled under various names: free market economics, monetarism, commercialisation, financialisation. At its core is competition as the basis of human relations and the market as the best way of allocating resources. To allow the market to work, it reduces the ability of the State to interfere, regulate or control. It treats citizens as consumers, dividing them up into winners, who must be encouraged by tax cuts and wealth accumulation, and losers, who fail through their own fault and lack of motivation. Thus, inequality becomes a virtue and unemployment a choice, not an unfairness to be minimised.

So, in the early 1980s, two new governments, Conservative in Britain, Labour in New Zealand, inspired by this philosophy, set out to give it flesh by demolishing the post-World

War II settlement of managed exchange rates, welfare states and Keynesian demand management to maintain full employment. They worked by rolling back the State, privatising state enterprises, drastically reducing higher tax rates, making taxation more regressive, and in Britain by breaking the unions, something done later in New Zealand by the following National government. Less successfully, they extended the reforms into the areas of health and education with payment by results, price systems and competitive league tables. All this was excused as reviving the economy. There was no alternative.

Britain and New Zealand were marched down neoliberalism's dead-end street for most of the time I was the member of the UK Parliament, for Grimsby. It was a long, frustrating period, because parliament could do so little to call a halt. Fortunately, having lost many of its old powers to the media, the House of Commons has become an adult education centre, bringing some of the best brains in Britain to inform and educate the minority of MPs stimulated by ideas. This benefit was boosted for me by the opportunity of working with stimulating colleagues like Bryan Gould, Michael Meacher, John Mills, Prem Sikka and John McDonnell. I am grateful to have had it.

Grateful too to the University of Canterbury, which awarded me one of their excellent Visiting Canterbury Fellowships, giving me the opportunity to return, like Rip

Van Winkle, to the Political Science Department which I'd helped to start half a century ago. There in 2016 I taught a summer school. My lectures formed the nucleus of this book.

My thanks also go to Bronwyn Hayward, the current head of the Department of Political Science and International Relations, who went out of her way to help me with the lectures and illustrate them by video material, which wasn't available in what I continue to think of as the good old days. I would express my gratitude too to the students who took the course, though they might feel that sympathy was more appropriate.

I also thank Catherine Montgomery of the Canterbury University Press, who took up the idea of the book, gave me help above and beyond the call of duty in revising it, and appointed Ric Stevens, who did an excellent job as editor, fact-checker and manager of the book. My thanks too to Stan Rodger, who read the first draft and helped me to avoid mistakes about New Zealand politics. I owe a special debt to my friend John Mills, who generously supported the publication financially.

My thanks to all of them, with the usual proviso that remaining faults are mine. I am a politician and a political scientist, so economists might quibble at my economic interpretations, but I can only wish they'd quibbled earlier and more loudly at the consequences of neoliberalism.

As the tide turns against neoliberalism, it's a good time to look at its failures in the hope that it might help the politicians to turn round and seek other ways to improve the lot of all the people. The story for both Britain and New Zealand is worth telling, because it hasn't been told before and might allow us to learn what happens when we govern by ideology rather than by simple common sense.

Austin Mitchell

Visiting Canterbury Fellow (Humanities),

University of Canterbury, December 2016

INTRODUCTION
A GAME OF TWO HALVES

Post-World War II politics in both Britain and New Zealand fall into two halves, each with different policy objectives, different systems of economic management and social imperatives, producing very different outcomes which have changed both nations.

The first half of the game, the good years, were the three and a half decades of economic growth and betterment which followed World War II. In Britain and New Zealand, as in the rest of the advanced world, the central purpose of government policy was to avoid another depression like that of the 1930s and reward the people by full employment and welfare. The key to achieving these objectives – following the economic theories of John Maynard Keynes, first published in 1936 – was economic growth, which sustained wellbeing, drove social and economic improvement and supported the welfare of all. The advanced countries achieved it; some spectacularly, others more slowly. Britain and New Zealand were among the laggards, but in both, as in every other advanced economy,

1

the lot of the people improved, their living standards rose and their household incomes grew. Looking back, it was an age of wellbeing.

The second half of the game, the three and a half decades from 1980, were the years of the Great Slowdown. These years were less happy, particularly in Britain and New Zealand. Neoliberal discipline replaced Keynesian expansion. Growth was lower, unemployment higher, wellbeing less and the steady improvement in household incomes stalled. This imposed a particular suffering on the poor and vulnerable, and turned politics sour, until eventually it became clear that the promises of improvement after the pain would not be delivered. Then the people pushed back against the market fundamentalism which had damaged their lot and the reign of neoliberalism came to an end. Not with a bang but with a prolonged whimper.

The first period, the never-had-it-so-good years, was the last stage of the long rise of the people which had begun in the 1890s. It was a post-war new age in which the brutalities and failures of capitalism were corrected and economic management was devoted to rewarding the people for the sufferings and sacrifices of war and depression. It was not a socialist but a socially democratic age, in which growth made everyone better off. Full employment and the welfare state protected the people from what the economist William Beveridge described, at the height of World War II, as the five "giant evils" facing society: want, disease, ignorance, squalor and idleness.

Growing up in that post-war period I benefitted from all this. My education was both good and free, not only through school but for eight years as a nearly perpetual university student. Job opportunities abounded. Unemployment was never a threat. Housing and food were cheap and for those who wanted more variety the Commonwealth was our oyster.

Like most people I assumed that governments had learned how to run the good society on the lines proposed by the economics of Keynes, so that this process of betterment would go on forever. Which made it a surprise when the post-war settlement in British politics began to fall apart in the 1970s, and an even bigger shock when opinion formers and political parties began to claim that the techniques and the institutions which had given us the affluent society had produced its nemesis. Economic management, they claimed, had to be returned to first principles, which in my eyes had been responsible for the pre-war Great Depression.

This was the start of the neoliberal revolution. It was carried out by the Conservative Party under Margaret Thatcher in Britain and by the Labour Party under Roger Douglas in New Zealand. The State, which social democrats had seen as the manager of the economy and the protector of the people, was now said to be the cause of the problems. It had to be cut back to give priority to the private sector and hand management to markets, which would be better at allocating resources. Public spending, much of it providing for the needs of the people, had to be cut back to give tax cuts to the better off, the drivers of enterprise and investment. Then the benefits would trickle down to the people instead of sustaining a dependency culture of subsidised idleness. The money supply, previously determined by the needs of the economy, had to be controlled to stop inflation.

All this came as a shock. Yet it quickly became an orthodoxy, changing government priorities and reshaping the economy. I had been elected to the British Parliament as MP for Grimsby but instead of improving the post-war settlement I had to switch to fighting to defend it. The following decades became a fighting retreat against neoliberalism, which transferred my efforts to picket lines as well as parliament, protesting the death of fishing, the cuts in steel, the breaking of the miners and the wasting of the manufacturing base which had supported Britain for so long. A job I had hoped would be positive turned negative.

Resistance was futile, though gradually the neoliberal surge petered out, only to be revived by the Great Recession of 2008. This had a bigger impact in Britain than in New Zealand. In the UK it was used to administer another dose of neoliberal medicine in the form of austerity, aimed at rolling back the State and punishing the people for the follies of the bankers. Not understanding the importance Keynes's multiplier effect had in stimulating the post-war economy, neoliberals claimed that public investment drove out private investment, so cutting it back would free up the private sector to invest and grow. In fact, it created a downward multiplier.

Horrified by the increase in debt to save the financial system, the UK's chancellor of the exchequer, George Osborne, didn't realise that the only way to cope with debt is to grow the economy to bear it. He cut everything back so the burden pressed more heavily. New Zealand managed to avoid all of this not because its government was more enlightened but because the impact of the Great Recession was less and the electorate had already revolted against the attempt to extend neoliberalism from the economy into the social area and told the politicians "enough is enough".

Britain and New Zealand should be studied together. Politically they were drifting apart but for three decades both were world leaders in the rush to neoliberalism. Both were held out by right-thinking Right-wingers as shining examples of the benefit of an old ideology re-polished and presented as new. Both marched with a similar determination down the same dead-end street; call it Milton Friedman Street. Both suffered the same consequences, though New Zealand suffered less because it did less damage to the industry which paid its way in the world: farming. Britain damaged its manufacturing industry far more deeply.

New Zealand began its march more enthusiastically

than Britain but realised its futility and called it to a halt much earlier. Britain, cushioned by North Sea oil and with a more deferential democracy, went on marching to futility far too long and suffered much greater damage, but by 2016 it too began to flag. The referendum on membership of the European Union produced a majority for Brexit, which was in fact a protest against both austerity and globalisation. This forced out George Osborne, the Svengali of neoliberalism, changed the government and turned the march in another direction. The long march down Dead-End Street was over, though in neither country was there any clear sense of where it should be directed instead.

CHAPTER ONE

THE WORLD WE LOST

THE THREE DECADES BETWEEN the Bretton Woods agreement in 1944 and President Nixon's decision to opt out of that settlement, as it began to crumble under the twin pressures of inflation and union militancy, were termed by the French "Les Trente Glorieuses" – for those of us privileged enough to live in what we were beginning to call the advanced world. The steady economic growth, rising living standards and growing equality occurred as more people, and more nations, shared the benefits of a process that (apart from a few disregarded gloom-mongering economists like Friedrich Hayek and Milton Friedman) governments and people assumed would go on forever. They thought it would create what John Maynard Keynes prophesied would be a world of less work, greater leisure and ever more prosperity.

The new order was shaped by men determined not to repeat the disasters of the Great Depression. The high unemployment, poverty, beggar-my-neighbour tariffs, protectionism and intense competition for slices of a shrinking cake had to be eliminated. These would be replaced by a new settlement, both internal and international, of co-operation, trade growth and welfare, which would protect the people and eliminate cut-throat competition by replacing cuts and deflation with growth and improvement. A new dawn was breaking with the post-war peace. The economic and social balances were tilted towards the people and away from the rampant capitalism that had caused the failings of the 1930s.

Internationally this new settlement was built by the Bretton Woods agreement, creating the International Monetary Fund to support and restructure economies through temporary difficulties and a World Bank to finance development. Both were to underpin a regime of fixed exchange rates designed to stop competitive devaluations and provide a stable basis for increased trade. Sterling lost its position as the world's reserve currency and was replaced by the US dollar, backed by the gold reserves in Fort Knox, Kentucky.

This new international framework provided the basis for an internal settlement which was at its best in Britain, moving a decade behind New Zealand to a benevolent welfare state, with a National Health Service, a planned economy in which failing industries were nationalised and restructured, and Keynesian demand management to ensure and maintain full employment. This was seen as the paramount objective of policy, so that human resources would not be wasted as they had been in the 1930s. Here was a new, social democratic world built by Labour, but carried on largely unchanged by their opponents, the National Party in New Zealand and the Conservative Party in Britain. The Conservatives' leader, Harold Macmillan, told the people in 1957 they had "never had it so good". This was ungrammatical but true, as growth improved living standards and enriched the people.

On these two bases, a new world regime and a welfare society, our two benevolent states set out to provide a better life for their people as the disciplines and stringencies of war were slowly relaxed. Full employment improved the people's lot, welfare states assuaged their problems, massive house-building programmes stimulated growth and gave them homes, free education and a school leaving age set at 15 educated them. Economic growth at between 2 and 3 percent in both Britain and New Zealand made them better off. Ministers began to claim that the standard of living would double in the next 25 years.

Within this common framework each nation developed in its own way. In Britain hire purchase produced a "live now pay later" lifestyle, television and bingo made Britons the best-entertained nation in the world and incomes rose steadily to pay for it all. Affluent Britain was contented. As A.J.P. Taylor put it at the end of his magisterial history of modern Britain, *English History 1914–1945*, published in 1965, "Few [now] sang 'England Arise'. But England had risen all the same."

The risen nation was complacent. Complacency is a British disease. The former imperial power (retired) still suffered from imperial delusions which had lingered on as Britain lost its empire but failed to find a new role. Britons didn't care. They'd won the war. They'd made the world fit for democracy, and for British cars to break down in. Whatever the evidence, people and governments shared the delusions of greatness and the over-confidence of empire, as if Britannia still ruled the waves and Britain remained a great power.

The result was imperial overload, as Britain assumed commitments it could no longer afford. Because of the Cold War it shouldered a greater defence burden than any of its competitors. It developed its own A and H bombs and tried to build the expensive missile and aircraft systems to deliver them. It kept military and naval forces east of Suez. It fought wars in Korea, Egypt, Kenya, Malaya, Brunei, Aden and Sarawak, all of which drained money and investment from the industrial economy which paid the nation's way in the world, and it kept the pound over-valued to do so.

New Zealand's economy was simpler, dependent on growing one crop, grass, and exporting the produce of the animals that ate it and the All Blacks who played rugby on it. Smaller, more classless and ever more practical, it shared the mother country's delusions because it felt itself to be, and was, British. A nation of largely British stock depended on British trade, British ships, British goods, British cars, British capital,

British wool and butter buyers, and the British market with which New Zealand did 75 percent of its trade. New Zealand was a British farm inconveniently placed in the distant South Pacific, where it felt itself to be what it had aspired to be for more than a century – a better Britain.

CHAPTER TWO

THE SEARCH FOR NEW MATES

THE STRAINS AND STRESSES on a post-war settlement that had been so successful in the 1940s and 1950s inevitably produced a search for new ideas and approaches. The people were still enjoying the ride, their lot was still improving, but "thinking politicians" and public intellectuals, both more numerous and vociferous in Britain than in New Zealand, began to worry about the problems. From the late 1950s and through the 1960s, a search began for new approaches and new ways of boosting growth.

In New Zealand, Keynesian orthodoxy still prevailed but its exponents, like economist Frank Holmes and the short-lived National Development Council, began to urge more investment and a search for new markets. In Britain, Michael Shanks in his 1961 book *The Stagnant Society* pointed to the need for faster economic growth. The former intelligence officer, historian and publisher Peter Calvocoressi empha-sised the problem of imperial overstretch, and economists on the Left began to discuss import controls and the need for planning in the style which was so successful in France. They were seeking to boost a British industry which, as military and economic historian Correlli Barnett pointed out, was old-fashioned, underinvested, complacent, and unmodernised. Others lamented the dominance of the trade unions, arguing that the shop stewards were far too powerful and out of control.

A babble of ideas and suggestions developed but one theme emerged as more important, and more straightforward, than the rest. The six European countries that had come together to form a Common Market – France, Belgium, Italy, Luxembourg, the Netherlands and West Germany – were all growing faster than slow, stagnant Britain. Enthusiasts put this success down not so much to French planning, or to German investment and continuous improvement, but to access to a bigger open market. If Britain were to join too, then it would share that success and get the faster growth that everyone wanted and that Labour in opposition, and later in the decade in power, promised to deliver. Labour MP and author Tony Crosland's devastating revisionism in *The Future of Socialism* had persuaded the party that socialism is about equality, not public ownership or greater welfare. Growth, he argued, was the way to deliver it. Everything Labour promised in 1964 depended on growth – indeed, the famous slogan "Let's Go with Labour" should really have been "Let's Grow with Labour".

14

Growth was required and joining the Common Market was preached as the way to get it. The arguments were simplistic, like so much of British economic thinking. British industry would benefit from the cold shower of competition in the same way as public school chaps were invigorated by the cold showers then de rigueur in their schools. The slow-growing British economy would be hitched on to faster European growth and British industry would be boosted by access to a wider market. None of this was true. Economics explained by fables about the family or seen as national physical fitness tests are usually rubbish, and governmental thinking about the Common Market certainly was. Cold showers can be fatal for a patient with pneumonia, and success in a larger market depends on a competitive exchange rate and a powerful exporting sector. These were exactly the areas where Britain was weakest. No matter. Europe was beginning to look like the answer to the country's emerging problems.

Conservative Prime Minister Harold Macmillan, who came to power in 1957, was the first to attempt to turn preference into policy. After the war, Winston Churchill had talked romantic guff about European unity but the old imperialist's heart was really with the Commonwealth and Empire. Macmillan was increasingly concerned about the complacency of British industry and its preference for the cosy home market, instead of competing in the world. The great actor-manager who posed as the last Edwardian was enough of a populist to see that Britain would decline and that the Commonwealth would become less useful, as either a force or a market, as colonies and dominions became independent and developed their own industries.

Something had to be done. For Macmillan that something was for Britain to become a member of the Common Market. After the 1959 election he began to take a more serious interest. Britain had declined to become involved in the initial moves to a coal and steel community and its participation in the initial negotiations for the Common Market had been restricted to an observer role. Although one of the Board of Trade negotiators, Shaun Stewart, saw that the French did not want the British as part of the club, few others saw this, for the British attitude towards Europe was, and always had been, one of condescension. Britain had won the war and liberated from fascism those funny Europeans without the Westminster system. Ministers assumed that the UK's participation would be received with gratitude as an infusion of wisdom and leadership. The Rolls Royce machine of the British civil service, the cream of the country's hand-polished brains, would quickly be running the outfit, and her politicians would have another bigger and better stage to strut on than that of the crumbling Commonwealth. They would offer to a grateful Europe the leadership and wisdom which had made Britain the world power it was ceasing to be.

These delusions of fading grandeur were punctured after months of haggling which brought out the skills of the

French civil servants and the determination of her politicians to dominate the Common Market. French president Charles de Gaulle said a grand "*Non*" to Britain in January 1963. He wanted the original six Common Market countries to be welded together more tightly and the structures settled down before bringing in British complications. He also saw Britain not only as a nuisance with its Commonwealth, but as an American Trojan horse, which of course it was, given its increasing dependence on the US. De Gaulle's vision was a powerful Europe based on a new Franco-German alliance acting as an intermediary between the Cold War antagonists, the US and Russia. Why complicate that by bringing in Britain with all its problems?

The veto destroyed Macmillan's plans, his solution to Britain's problems, and, effectively, his government. After his "Super Mac" image was destroyed by the John Profumo sex scandals of 1963, his only hope was to buy electoral support through the biggest ever dose of "go" in the old "stop-go" cycle. This was the boom of Reginald Maudling's 1963 "expansion without inflation" budget, which fell apart the following year and produced the biggest overseas deficit seen so far.

In 1964, the incoming Labour government under Harold Wilson learned a trick which was to become increasingly familiar in matters European. It stood on its head. When Macmillan had first proposed membership of the Common Market, Hugh Gaitskell, Labour's leader from 1955 to 1963, opposed entry as a betrayal of the Commonwealth and of a thousand years of history. Within two years of achieving power, Gaitskell's successor Wilson revived Macmillan's plans and resumed negotiations for entry. Only to face the same abject failure. De Gaulle preferred the powerful Franco-German alliance to Wilson's slippery diplomacy.

There matters rested until everything was changed by the failure of Wilson's efforts to achieve growth, the death of de Gaulle (who was replaced by the more accommodating Georges Pompidou) and the advent of a new Tory prime minister, Ted Heath. He was the first (and only) British prime minister to show a cool disregard for the US and an enthusiastic preference for Europe, which he saw as the answer to Britain's problems. More than that, Heath made entry to Europe the central policy of the Conservative Party and the crucial purpose of his government when he unexpectedly won the 1970 election. It was certainly the only part of his programme which succeeded.

Heath resumed negotiations, only to find that the Common Market had hardened in its original mould as a deal between the industrial interests of Germany, wanting a larger open market, and the protectionist instincts of French agriculture. The latter was a framework into which it was difficult to fit Britain, with the worldwide interests of the City of London, its uncompetitive industry and its dependence on cheap food from the Commonwealth.

Heath's desperation to join the club made him ready to

sacrifice several sacred cows on the European altar. Among these sacrifices were the interests of the Commonwealth, particularly New Zealand, which got a restricted transitional entry for its produce for a while. Albion can be very perfidious when it's scared: Heath sacrificed the housewife, who lost the cheap food Britain had enjoyed for so long, and he sacrificed the fishing industry, which was forced to give European fleets "equal access to a common resource" while the rest of the world was taking 200-mile limits. Fishing was, in a civil servant's words later leaked from the Scottish Office, "expendable". It was duly expended.

So, Britain began its new relationship on terms less than adequate. It passed the European Communities Act of 1972, which gave Common Market laws and regulations automatic force in Britain without the intervention or the consent of parliament. It immediately became a net contributor to the Market's costs, because its finances were based on levies on food and produce coming in from outside, which Britain depended on more than any other country. Object achieved, Heath was happy to carry the burdens because he believed in European union, but having promised the "wholehearted consent" of the British people to his grand project he refused to seek it through offering the nation a referendum. Nor would he give the people any other say, because he knew that they'd reject the change. They had to be content with a parliamentary vote for membership. Heath won by the narrow margin of 309 to 301 votes, achieved only because the Labour Party split. Both parties were divided on membership but a majority of the Conservative Party were joined by 69 Labour rebels, enough to pass the legislation.

However loud the British chorus of grumbles at an unequal and unsatisfactory marriage, the issue was concreted over for the next 30 years. Or rather, given Brussels' penchant for grandiose architecture, it was consecrated in marble. As the marble monuments grew, so the problems emerged. Britain had hitched to faster growth only to find that growth slowed as the couplings tightened. Donald Stokes, the Chief Executive of British Motor Corporation, and other leaders of British industry, had assured the country that Europe would buy British. It didn't. What had been a surplus in trade with the six founding nations before Britain went in, quickly became a large and growing deficit afterwards. European goods were better, and it is easier to penetrate a small market from a big one than vice versa. Britain was duly penetrated.

Skilled though Britain's elite civil servants were, their European counterparts were more so. The French were smarter, more commercially minded, and better politicians, having largely run their country whereas the British civil service merely advised. The French were also committed to pursuing national interest. The Franco-German partnership which de Gaulle had welded was so dominant that the Brits were unable to interpose themselves or even influence the agenda. Yet when the British complained and grumbled (as was becoming a national habit) their new partners were well justified in telling them that they couldn't join a rugby club and then expect to play cricket. The club could change its colours, and regularly did so like a chameleon, painting itself red to tell trade unionists it would help and protect them, blue to reassure Conservatives that it was a capitalist club. But it couldn't and wouldn't change its substance.

What it could do, however, was search for a new dynamic. The Common Market and particularly the Brussels bureaucracy which managed it had an inbuilt drive to ever closer union. By the 1970s this was beginning to stall as new entrants like Britain and Denmark diluted the old relationship and electorates began to make it clear that they were unlikely to consent to any further dilution of national sovereignty to achieve a goal which looked increasingly distant, even unnecessary.

So Brussels began to look to currency union as the new driver to federal union. A common currency would produce economic convergence and require federal institutions, like a European bank, a European budget and probably a common economic policy, leading to union through the back door and without the need for electoral consent. Roy Jenkins, the president of the European Commission, backed this fateful step. The Common Market changed its name to the European Economic Community and set up an exchange rate mechanism (ERM) to lead to a common currency. Europe began to tread a very dangerous path, with disastrous consequences to emerge later.

While Britain was fitting into a new partnership, only to find that the promised economic benefits didn't come, New Zealand, the partner it had cast adrift, was being forced to look to new markets. It focused, as Britain had, on a new relationship, the initiative for which came from outside, from Australia, rather than internally from New Zealand's own political elite and leaders. In 1965, Jack Marshall, the New Zealand deputy prime minister with responsibility for overseas trade, had negotiated a partial free trade arrangement with Australia. In 1980, the Australian deputy prime minister Doug Anthony began to propose a closer economic relationship with New Zealand and found a ready response from Hugh Templeton, the New Zealand trade minister. Templeton felt that "the case was coming out strongly for closer economic relations that would provide support for broader-based industry. A larger market of 20 million would then encourage rationalisation and modernisation in both countries."

New Zealand manufacturers expressed their doubts, fearful of more intense competition, as did Prime Minister Robert Muldoon, who preferred an insulated little New Zealand as a better stage to strut on. Muldoon prevaricated and delayed – the time was never ripe – but ultimately, he was persuaded by Templeton to go along with the deal. It was finally (and belatedly) ratified in 1983 with the liberalisation of 80 percent of the trade between the two countries, dairy entry for New Zealand and a transition period for the New Zealand car assembly industry. Closer Economic Relations (CER) was a simpler agreement than Britain's with the Common Market, made no proposals for the "ever closer union" which drove Europe towards federalism, and was far less grandiose, because it concentrated on balanced trade concessions rather than any completely open door.

Harder haggling and Muldoon's caution had secured a better deal for New Zealand than Britain had from Europe and, unlike the Common Market, CER was simply a trading relationship, not a commitment to build a new unity. So though New Zealand manufacturing was weakened and a good deal of production shifted to Australia, the trade was better balanced. Some firms, such as Crown Lynn, went bust, though it was over-extended anyway; some, such as Fisher & Paykel, transferred some production (such as fridges) to Australia. Others transferred all of it and not much came the other way, but Australia invested in New Zealand and the two countries worked and developed more closely together.

New Zealand was shifting away from the economic relationship with Britain. The limpet was seeking not a new rock but an arrangement which was less pretentious than Britain's with the Common Market, and was simply part of the search for new markets which Britain had precipitated.

Both countries were searching for new approaches and new arrangements to ease the problems of slow growth and the tightening balance-of-payments constraint. Yet neither had found them in new partnerships and new markets. Indeed, both suffered damage from these new arrangements, though New Zealand was more successful in seeking out new markets while Britain lost them and sank into its trade with the European Union rather than the wider world. The trade imbalances had been compounded not reduced. Growth and the ability to pay the nation's way were reduced by the impact of new competition in manufacturing. The search for solutions had to go on because the first and simplest attempt to regenerate and improve hadn't yielded the benefits prophesied.

CHAPTER THREE

THE END OF THE GOLDEN WEATHER

NEITHER BRITAIN NOR NEW ZEALAND was regenerated or boosted by its new association, Britain's with the European six, New Zealand's with Australia. The post-war settlement, the affluent societies it sustained, and the Keynesian demand management for growth still remained the norm in both countries, but it was performing less adequately and under increasing strain. Yet it didn't just fade away under the pressures of inflation, industrial unrest and balance-of-payments problems. Its structures, intact into the 1970s, were deliberately destroyed in the early 1980s by a revolution which economists might describe as a new economics, and social scientists as moving the social balances from workers and the people to business and wealth. However, a post-mortem on the benevolent state must, sadly, lead us to accept that its friends – the trade unions in Britain, the Labour Party in New Zealand – also contributed to its demise.

By the 1970s, the welfare society was no longer in its full flourishing vigour of the never-had-it-so-good years. People who had become addicted to growth were beginning to ask for more and faster growth than the machine could deliver. The trade unions were becoming more difficult to control. Incomes policies were introduced to check inflation but succeeded only partially. Balance-of-payments problems reduced hopes for steady growth and led to a lurching process of stop-go. Then, on top of all these strains, came the great oil price hike of 1974–75. This was a deeply damaging body blow to both economies and a transfer of power, growth and demand from the oil-consuming West to the mainly Middle Eastern Organisation of the Petroleum Exporting Countries (OPEC). The result was accelerating inflation.

Yet growth continued, though at a lower rate than that enjoyed by Europe, Japan or the younger dragons. It was not beyond the wit of governments in Britain and New Zealand, even if they could not solve the problems, to at least bring the two countries through the difficulties and find new ways to sustain the settlement for a better day.

In Britain, Prime Minister Edward Heath's vain struggle to control the unions ended in a miners' strike and a three-day work week in 1974. One Conservative, Patrick Jenkin, bravely asked the nation to make sacrifices by using their toothbrushes in the dark; he became notorious when it was revealed his own toothbrush was electric. Chancellor of the Exchequer Anthony

Barber denounced the miners for holding the country to ransom. Heath decided to hold an election in February 1974 to ask, "Who governs Britain?"

Not you, matey, was Britain's answer. Heath then tried for a coalition with the Liberals to stay in power but their leader, Jeremy Thorpe, would not sustain a rejected government. Soon after this, Thorpe faced his own difficulties, being blackmailed by an ex-lover, Norman Scott. This affair . turned to farce when a supporter trying to help the leader by shooting the blackmailer, hired an incompetent gunman who shot Scott's dog Rinka instead, producing a louder lament from animal lovers than if he'd shot the rejected lover.

Heath's failure brought Labour and Harold Wilson back to power, a victory confirmed by a second election in October 1974. Labour's approach was collaborative, even corporatist, based on a social contract between Labour and the trade unions under which government agreed to boost social spending to cushion the impact of the oil price increase. In return, the unions agreed to a voluntary incomes policy, developed and enforced by them, in which everyone got the same pay increase of £3 a week.

It worked. Manufacturing decline slowed. The number of strikes and stoppages fell. Inflation came down. The Liberals, under a new leader, David Steel, agreed to a Lib-Lab pact to sustain the government on motions of confidence and supply. Labour started to win by-elections; a turning of the tide, a symptom of which was my own victory in the Grimsby by-election of April 1977. Growth revived. By 1978 it looked as though Labour could win the great prize both political parties were now competing for: to be in power when the newly-developed North Sea oil came on stream to boost the economy and solve the balance-of-payments problem.

New Zealand, hit by greater difficulties, was also coming through, though the ride was bumpier. The Labour government elected in 1972 had begun to make the country a more liberal society. It began the search for new markets, but then ran into huge difficulties. The oil price increase boosted inflation. The party's inspiring leader, Norman Kirk, fell ill, became paranoid, and died in 1973. The National Party dumped its leader, Jack Marshall, a man too nice for New Zealand politics, and brought in Robert Muldoon, a mean-spirited exponent of counter-punching and going for the enemy's gut, of whom a common saying had it: "No one's perfect except Rob, who's a perfect bastard." That quality soon showed in his bitter onslaught, backed by the blue-collar conservatives he dubbed Rob's Mob, on Labour's government and its new leader, Bill Rowling (another man too nice for New Zealand politics). They also outbid Labour's far-sighted plans for a national superannuation scheme, which Muldoon countered with a National Party superannuation policy that was more generous in cash terms immediately, but less useful in the long term.

Mob rule worked: National came to power in 1975 to offer Rob's solutions. Muldoon was the last of New Zealand's big spenders and he set out to intensify post-war Keynesian and welfare policies. Those opponents who weren't scared of him hated him. Neither emotion should conceal his real achievements. As a Keynesian big spender, he determined that the people should not suffer. He kept welfare spending high, particularly on superannuation. He later tackled inflation with a two-year total freeze on price and pay increases, between 1982 and 1984. He even revived the efforts of the former Secretary of Industries and Commerce, Bill Sutch, whom the National government had forced into retirement in the mid-1960s, to initiate industrial development and import substitution. In the late 1970s, this was exemplified by Think Big – major projects in oil, gas, steel and aluminium. All were predicated on the assumption that energy prices would continue to increase. They didn't.

The 1970s were difficult years. The British and New Zealand economies were still in comparative decline in an advanced world. Both were falling behind and their governments had to turn to tougher measures to bring them through. Under Muldoon New Zealand ran into massive deficits, both internal and external. Yet both were coping. Just. Growth was still going on. People were becoming richer, though the difficulties and the tough measures taken to deal with them were generating grumbles, dissatisfaction and a search for new solutions, and new ways of running and repairing what were becoming two rickety ships.

In both countries, the older generation which had endured depression and war was better prepared to accept the disciplines and privations. Growth may have been slow but was better than anything they had experienced in the past. But the younger generation, the Baby Boomers born in a post-war world, were not. They were less amenable to the disciplines and had higher expectations. Where their parents had travelled overseas in uniform in order to kill foreigners, Baby Boomers travelled for fun and not only liked what they saw but admired the people they met, particularly in France, Germany and Italy. For young Kiwis on "OE" every prospect pleased. Even Australia.

The higher standards of living, the competition to serve the consumer, the array of goods and services made the Boomers feel like hicks from the sticks, a feeling I remember well from my occasional visits to Australia for conferences where I was condescended to by better-paid, higher-flying Australian academics, and where I goggled at bowling alleys, drive-in cinemas, bikinis and Italian restaurants. Kiwis abroad loved the new consumer societies and came home wanting change and the excitement it offered, in much the same way as British socialists like Tony Crosland had returned from America keen to harness American dynamism for socialism.

Business, too, was beginning to grumble, though more loudly and to even greater effect since it controlled the newspapers and had the ear of government. In the 1950s, business and the wealthy had grudgingly accepted the new order because Keynesian economic management had kept demand up, competition minimal and home markets comfortable; by the 1970s they were protesting about high taxation, excessive regulation, trade union power and wild fluctuations in demand. In New Zealand, all this became more bitter and focused on Muldoon, whose price-and-incomes freeze reduced profits. It so angered Bob Jones, a hotelier and property developer, that he decided to abandon the National Party and start his own, the New Zealand Party, in 1983.

These were practical problems but the third source of discontent was theoretical, with the rejection of the policy approaches on which the whole settlement was based. Its intellectual foundations were being undermined by new philosophies blowing in from the Windy City of Chicago in the form of neoliberal, free-market economics, a heady cocktail which involved several sub-schools, recently analysed by Jane Kelsey in her 2015 book *The FIRE Economy*, describing a system based mainly on the financial, insurance and real estate sectors. The basic beliefs were that markets are more rational and more efficient than state management, and that cutting taxes on the wealthy will not only liberate energies and investments but increase government revenues. This was a claim justified (and illustrated) by much use of the Laffer curve, purporting to show that higher taxes reduce revenue when the rich feel themselves to be over-taxed and seek havens elsewhere. Lower taxes would perhaps bring home Elton John, Fleetwood Mac and all the other pop heroes who'd gone into tax exile. Keynesian demand management, it was argued, was stoking inflation and should be replaced by supply side measures to break the shackles and boost the economy. Inflation would be stopped by controlling the money supply, an easy way to stop too much money pursuing too few goods.

Here was a whole new approach, argued by Milton Friedman, implemented by Alan Greenspan at the US Federal Reserve (the FED) and popularised by Ayn Rand in her boring novels, which I was amazed to find were actually read in New Zealand, not just used to frighten socialists. Presented as something new, it was in fact a respray of the failed approaches of the 1920s and a revival of the discredited libertarianism of Friedrich Hayek, now justified by extolling the dynamism of Hong Kong, and by homely analogies such as Friedman's little story that roaring inflation in the southern states during the American Civil War was immediately halted when Union forces destroyed the printing presses of the Confederate mint. This appealed to the prejudices of business and politicians like Margaret Thatcher (converted to the new thinking by her Conservative colleague Sir Keith Joseph, nicknamed the "Mad Monk") by giving them an intellectual justification for things they'd been longing to do anyway, like tilting social balances back to wealth and breaking the power of the trade unions.

The philosophy was first brought home to me on a British parliamentary delegation to Brazil, where a Conservative MP and I watched hundreds of labourers loading scores of boats on the Amazon with supplies to go up river. It was a chaos of carriers worthy of a photograph by Sebastião Salgado, the famous Brazilian photographer of toil. The Tory, seeing order emerge out of chaos, sighed, "There's the magic of the market." I saw only exploitation of overburdened and underpaid workers by greedy vessel owners. As the new economics emerged and were trumpeted by conservatives, the Left failed to realise the seriousness of the challenge. We described Margaret Thatcher as Attila the Hen or Catherine the Great of Finchley, and laughed at her manner of speaking to people as if their dog had just died. Instead of arguing it out we told ourselves it would never work and chortled at her prescriptions.

Reactions in New Zealand were not dissimilar, except that there was no one to laugh at, only Muldoon to hate. Roger Douglas, the brightest spark and the only new thinker in the opposition ranks, unveiled new ideas in his book *There's Got to Be a Better Way* in 1980. Some of them were very sensible, like a devaluation to make New Zealand more competitive, and state stimulus to new developments, such as more carpet factories and other exporting producers in every town.

Leading economist Suzanne Snively had assembled a group of her colleagues to discuss economics with Douglas, but they soon found he was losing interest. He was listening instead to Treasury, which had absorbed the new ideas and policies coming in from Chicago, and then Britain, and which hated Muldoon because he never listened to them. Under Bernie Galvin, Treasury had set up a group, Economics 2, to set out what they would like to do if Muldoon were to fall under a bus. Doug Andrew was the Treasury representative advising the opposition leader's office, but he was propagating their new ideology in the Labour Party, particularly to Roger Douglas. It was pretty unconstitutional for a government department to re-educate a political party in this way but Douglas, always a sucker for big ideas, took them up like a convert to a new fundamentalist religion. Treasury became his new priesthood, educators, supporters; even his powerhouse.

So, by the late 1970s, early 1980s, the old order was under severe strain and becoming increasingly difficult to maintain. Business was dissatisfied and new ideas were taking over the opposition parties, Conservative in the UK, Labour in New Zealand. Yet the post-war settlement could still have been repaired and renewed by a more co-operative approach like Australia's Accord or the German partnership system. The electorate grumbled but had no great desire for a new system of economic management. Much of the new philosophy appeared impractical and unworkable. It would be wrong to argue that neoliberalism prevailed by popular acclaim or that there was a massive revolt against the post-war settlement. The new order was imposed. And it came to power by accident.

In New Zealand, its chance came thanks to Muldoon's failing capacities and growing inflexibility, both well illustrated by Hugh Templeton in *All Honourable Men*, an account of the Muldoon cabinets in which he served. There Templeton describes Muldoon's bullying, his increasing isolation from a cabinet and caucus he dominated, his failing judgement and his propensity to indulge the factor which undermined so many New Zealand prime ministers since "King" Dick Seddon 80 years earlier: the desire to strut around the wider world, play the statesman and get away from all the strains and hard work of party management and crude party politics. To this should be added Muldoon's growing intemperance, caused by a combination of drink and diabetes. This sad picture of a failing giant culminated, in July 1984, in self-immolation.

Strain had grown as the two-year wage and price freeze ran on. Muldoon's majority, now reduced to one, was threatened by Marilyn Waring, a courageous National MP determined to vote for Labour MP Richard Prebble's motion opposing visits by nuclear ships. Sue Wood, the National Party's president, was in the course of dissuading her when Muldoon burst in and brutally tore his backbencher to shreds, which reinforced her determination. The die was cast. Muldoon, drunk by the evening, hauled the governor-general out of a cosy little dinner party in Government House to get him to agree to a snap election, and went on TV, still slurring, to call it. The Schnapps election, some described it; called in booze, repented in sobriety. Given the crisis, the near-collapse of the dollar and the government's disarray, Muldoon was bound to lose in 1984. Labour came in with neoliberal prescriptions all ready in Roger Douglas's briefcase and set out in Treasury's outline of the policies it wanted in *Economic Management*, its analysis of the problems and its guidance for the new government.

In Britain, neoliberalism's advent to power was equally accidental. By 1978, the economy was reviving well. Labour was ahead in the polls and could have hung on until October 1979, by which time the North Sea oil would have been flowing. Or, even better, the government could have called an early election with a good chance of winning, though by a small majority. But Jim Callaghan, always right on his small judgements but wrong on the big ones, decided to prolong his successful incomes policy and wait. It was a disastrous decision. The big unions couldn't hold the policy. Their members were in revolt for higher pay, both in the well-paid car industry and the lower-paid health service. In 1979 they struck. Transport drivers, who had a stranglehold on the economy, stopped work. So did local authority and health service employees. Rubbish piled up in the streets and, the press claimed, bodies went unburied. This Winter of Discontent became a massive revolt by the workers against their government and the leadership of their unions. No Labour government could win an election in those circumstances. Labour lost. Jim Callaghan belatedly detected a massive sea change, which heralded the dawn of a new age. Margaret Thatcher came into Downing Street and read out a little homily from St Francis of Assisi – "Where there is discord, may we bring harmony..." – which she had written on a card earlier; she then put the card back in her handbag and took out the monetarist free-market policies, which brought that brief harmony to a bitter end.

Neoliberalism had triumphed in both countries, and not by any popular choice. It took the form of a new philosophy, one which, because it came via the minds of politicians – instinctive improvisers rather than economic theorists – was turned into concrete policies reflecting their prejudices and instincts. Collectively the resulting policies are called neoliberalism, but they really involved a whole set of approaches individually described as monetarism, free-market economics, liberalisation, commercialisation, financialisation and other less complimentary words. Better therefore to describe the separate strands and bring out their collective impact.

The basic assumption was that free markets operate more

effectively and efficiently than state control or regulation. People will be more powerful and democracy more effective if they are left to manage their own destinies, buy their public housing and shares in privatised businesses, and use the power of their own credit, rather than depending on the State or organising in unions, which create conflict, shackle enterprise and generate inflation. This can be eliminated by controlling the money supply rather than pandering to the unions or imposing an incomes policy. It follows, therefore, that private enterprise is better and more efficient than nationalised business, which is captured by producers, and that management skills are transferable: someone who has run a brewery can also run a hospital and the chief executive of a computer software firm will be equally good at running a university.

The rich are better drivers of growth and investment than the State, or so the story runs, and competition drives the desire to serve the public, rather than protecting the interests of the producers, which means that the rich should be energised by tax cuts. The philosophy of this belief in incentives was reverse Robin Hood. The second greatest Yorkshireman (after Captain Cook) had pioneered taking from the rich to give to the poor. Now that was to be thrown into reverse. The poor, it was clear to neoliberals, weren't working hard enough because the State had spoiled them by showering benefits and support on them. The rich were different:

they weren't working hard enough because they didn't have enough money to incentivise them to get out of bed to work and invest.

The solution was simple. Take the money from the poor, give it to the rich and everyone would be working more happily than the seven dwarfs. Both groups would be incentivised and the money would trickle down to the public without the intervention of the State taking its cut through progressive taxation. Beneficiaries would learn the joy of their own strength and independence rather than sinking into the torpor of dependency culture. Lower taxes would curtail the steady growth of the State by cutting off its oxygen. Basic to this whole approach is the belief that individual freedom increases as the role of the State reduces. Therefore, regulation must be soft-touch and preferably in the form of self-regulation (or chaps regulating chaps, as we see it in Britain), because public ownership is inefficient and tax a restraint on enterprise.

None of this is absolutely true. Some of it is wrong, as was proved when Jim Bolger, New Zealand's National Party prime minister for seven years in the 1990s, put business people in charge of the health service. When governments began to implement this programme, political opponents, some of whom half-believed in it, either made fun of it or confidently assumed it would fail. The social democratic assumptions of the welfare society had rusted, politicians had become sloppy in their thinking and Labour, lacking any strong ideology, had never educated its party or people about the frameworks and policies which had produced the improvements of the good years. Opposition proved to be an empty shell, easily crushed by the impressive new tank, while the electorate had simply voted in its habitual fashion to throw the bastards out without having the foggiest idea of what the bastards who replaced them had in mind.

Yet both sets of bastards had an enormous strength in the power of the elective dictatorship built on the first-past-the-post electoral system. Under it, the executive controls the legislature because it has a built-in majority to do what it wants. It controls caucus, caucus controls parliament and parliament can do anything except, as the old joke goes, change a man into a woman (although these days, if it wishes, it can supply the taxpayers' money to enable the operation to do that). Geoffrey Palmer, one of Labour's 1980s prime ministers, rightly called it *Unbridled Power?* in the title of his 1979 book, though when he re-issued the book after coming into power he dropped the question mark.

Governments drive a steamroller; it can be heckled (indeed that's the job of parliament and the opposition), but it can't be stopped. Ideally the driver will listen to suggestions about the route the steamroller should take. Some drivers wander all over the countryside, but now, inspired by neoliberalism, the drivers in New Zealand and the UK had a route map in their own heads and weren't prepared to consider alternative routes. Not only were they right, they considered, but there was no alternative. Thatcher used the phrase "There is no alternative" so often that people shortened it to "TINA". Tina ruled.

CHAPTER FOUR

THE WRECKING GANG ARRIVES

IN 1979 IN BRITAIN, and 1984 in New Zealand, neoliberals took over the driving seat of the governmental steamroller, determined to begin the demolition of the failing post-war settlement. They came to power by accident, because their opponents threw it away. They had little support for their programmes of free-market economics to swing the social balances away from workers to wealth. They took most people by surprise when they began their demolition job and had no mandate to bring the affluent years to an end. They won the elections in both countries because the public had voted in its usual way to throw out a failing government with no idea of what the opposition proposed to do. Oppositions don't win elections; governments lose them. In New Zealand, Robert Muldoon lost big time in 1984. The electorate wanted rid of him, but not the massive changes they were about to get from the incoming Labour government.

Both countries had problems: union power in Britain, a run on the dollar in New Zealand. Yet both could be dealt with by sensible policies and neither was enough to justify the revolution the new governments embarked on. Indeed, the first indications were that the old, well-tried methods would work. In Britain, on her election as prime minister in 1979, Margaret Thatcher read her little homily about harmony on the doorstep of 10 Downing Street with only a brief glance at her prompt card. In New Zealand, the charismatic Labour leader David Lange won the 1984 snap election with a manifesto drawn up by his deputy, Geoffrey Palmer, to cover two strands in the party's thinking: Roger Douglas's free-market ideas and Mike Moore's more corporate approach. Labour forced the departing and reluctant Prime Minister Muldoon into a sensible 20 percent devaluation to end a balance-of-payments crisis. The incoming Labour government then immediately called an "economic summit" to bring all sections together to work out a corporate agreement for developing the economy and getting back to growth.

These appearances were deceptive. Within a short time, Thatcher, the advocate of harmony, was plunging Britain into unprecedented strife, while in New Zealand the corporate hopes were chucked overboard and replaced by a full-scale onslaught on the State. The new people in the driving seat had got religion, a new ideology which drove them to use the steamrollers as a wrecking tool to destroy the post-war settlement which both incoming governments considered had outlived its usefulness.

As an aspiring woman who'd married a millionaire, Margaret Thatcher's ideology was a product of the upper-class prejudices of wealth. She had a distaste for unions, which she saw as enablers of inflation, which disturbed the established order. She took patriotic pride in a nation she saw as being undermined and humiliated by strikes, the Left and the intellectuals. Her constant question was whether someone was "one of us", the small band of right-thinking people who had seen the light.

Activist prime ministers are divisive. Thatcher was the most divisive ever. Adored by the Tory press and by people on the Right as the new Boadicea – a veritable "She who must be obeyed" – she was reviled on the Left. Critics outweighed the enthusiasts, at least until she displayed her courage and determination by winning back the Falkland Islands from Argentinian occupiers, against the inclination of many in her cabinet. Her public standing had collapsed after the shortest honeymoon poll lead in history but she was then buoyed by a tide of patriotic enthusiasm. The Thatcher enigma was best summed up by President Mitterrand of France, who described her as having "the eyes of Caligula but ... the mouth of Marilyn Monroe".

Love her or hate her, Margaret Thatcher was an artefact, the first British prime minister to be created and projected by a team. The Bell Pottinger public relations agency changed her image, softening her hair style and lowering her voice by an octave so she became less shrill. Christopher Fry inspired her jokes and aphorisms, like "the lady's not for turning", because she had no sense of humour herself. A team wrote her speeches and, most important of all, Bernard Ingham, a former Labour council candidate, proved to be the press secretary from heaven (but better still, since he came from Yorkshire). Knowing her mind and thinking more graphically than she did herself, he created the monster by making her confused prejudices more coherent, retailing her views in daily press conferences and building her image in the press.

The reality was less impressive, but she was adept at testing conventional civil service arguments, often to destruction. She probed the pompous, loved argument and debate, was abrasive in battle, but kind to staff and friends. It pleased me that she often replied to my letters telling her how to run the country with a handwritten postscript on the official bland reply, telling me exactly why I was wrong. They indicated that at least she had thought about the issue and understood the argument, which was more than I could say for many Labour ministers I wrote to.

Yet this bossy, domineering woman was also vulnerable. Her biographer, Charles Moore, said that she always knew she wasn't one of the club so no one would catch her if she fell. She never lost the fear that her government might fall apart, an insecurity known only to a few and which may have lain behind her overbearing behaviour in cabinet, as recorded, for instance, by Norman Fowler, a junior minister, in 1981: "Margaret accuses all government ministers of not having the first idea about what is going on … Margaret really cannot continue to treat everyone in this extraordinarily aggressive manner."

She didn't. A third of her first cabinet were "Wets", supporters of Ted Heath and the more compassionate conservatism of the past. They were led by the great compromiser, Willie Whitelaw, who set himself up as a wise father figure. But when he retired and the Wets were weeded out and replaced by courtiers her aggression focused on Michael Heseltine, a rival for the premiership, and Sir Geoffrey Howe, her docile chancellor and later foreign minister. She became more opinionated and, like most prime ministers, more and more convinced of her own rightness and less patient of opposition. The office generates hubris. She got it, a situation summed up by the joke about Thatcher entertaining her cabinet to dinner: She ordered roast beef from the waiter and was asked, "What about the vegetables?" "Oh," she replied, "they'll have roast beef too."

The revolution had begun slowly and cautiously in Britain. The pound was floated and exchange controls abolished. Value Added Tax (VAT), a consumption tax, was nearly doubled in 1979 to 15 percent, in defiance of an election promise not to do so. A particularly tough budget in 1981 harshly depressed the economy. Privatisation, given only a brief mention in the manifesto, started with motorway service stations, then British Petroleum and British Aerospace, moving on to British Airways then the great utilities of gas, power, water, British Telecom, airports, docks and railways. The attack on the unions, whose power she was determined to break, began with legislation restricting their powers to strike and requiring ballots before action.

Labour, in opposition, was baffled, certain that this unprecedented reversal of all the norms of the welfare society must end in tears but impotent to do anything about it beyond provide a national handkerchief. The elective dictatorship's steamroller drove it all through parliament, and the efforts of MPs like myself were transferred from the House to the picket lines, many and various, but all futile. Labour's reactions to privatisation began with proposals to take it all back, inevitably modified to taking back with compensation, then sulky silence as it became clear that so much had been sold we'd never be able to afford to take back anything much at all. Labour's critique then began to concentrate on the need for tough regulation of privatised monopolies. This, however, was an American skill, not one for the British Establishment, which preferred to let chaps regulate chaps, or for a government, aware that tough regulation would reduce the price at which the assets could be sold.

We were clear that it would never work. Indeed, monetarism, the effort to control inflation by controlling the money supply, did quickly fail. Monetarists had assumed that the money supply was exogenous and could be switched on and off like a tap. In fact, it is endogenous. The economy sucks in the money supply it needs. So turning the tap off withers the plant. The government discovered that it could only control the money supply by nationalising the banks, which issued 97 percent of the nation's credit. Since they were not prepared to do that, the obsession with M1, M2 and M3, the various measures of money supply, was quietly dropped in favour of rationing money by high interest rates.

This in turn compounded the new sickness of Dutch disease, the tendency first discovered by that country for the exchange rate to rise as domestic energy supplies (in their case gas, in Britain's North Sea oil) came on stream. Instead of going down, as Britain's declining competitiveness required, the pound rose to new heights, inflicting heavy damage on British manufacturing, reducing exports and boosting imports, leading to the de-industrialisation of the former workshop of the world and turning the balance of trade from surplus to deficit.

Because my constituency of Grimsby then produced caravans I swallowed my dislike of these lumbering monstrosities and went every year to the Caravan Show. A year after Thatcher took over I talked to the chief executive of Caravans International. Hearing that he was facing a decline of exports I asked him what he thought of Margaret Thatcher's economic policies. "Marvellous," he said, "at last management has the power to manage." Two years later he wasn't there. Caravans International had gone bust. The following year I wasn't there either. Grimsby's manufacturer had packed it in.

Perversely, ministers welcomed that process. The flood of imports kept people happy and concealed the damage being done to British manufacturing. The benefits of oil wealth could be portrayed as the result of the new policies. The decline of manufacturing and the basic industries which sustained it could be answered by the argument that phoenixes rise from ashes, so the more ashes created, the better the phoenixes' prospects. Unemployment, which had always been kept down in the past, leading to a boost to the economy whenever it threatened, was now used as a means of discipline. Ted Heath had been horrified when unemployment rose to a million in 1972 and had thrown everything into reverse to bring it down. Margaret Thatcher by 1983 had put it up to three million and more without qualms and Norman Lamont, a later chancellor of the exchequer, described it as "a price worth paying" (though not, of course, by him and his class). It was a necessary element of policy because it reduced inflation and disciplined the workers. Ministers began to talk of "a natural rate of unemployment", which was now claimed to be several points higher than in the affluent years.

This damped down the productive economy in much the same way as bloodletting had once been used to improve health, but it was an essential part of neoliberalism. It weakened the unions, a prime purpose of the Thatcher government, which viewed them not as partners as Labour had done but as "the enemy within". This came to fulfilment when the government took on and defeated the praetorian guard of the labour movement, the National Union of Mineworkers. They'd defeated Ted Heath and brought his government down in 1974 but Margaret Thatcher bided her time, accumulated coal stocks and, when she was ready, provoked the great miners' strike of 1984–85.

Arthur Scargill, the president of the miners' union who had taken over from the cautious, conciliatory Joe Gormley, was also spoiling for a fight. The pretext was provided by a leaked proposal to close 70 pits. This was part of a process to close small, uneconomic pits and transfer to larger mines, which had been going on for years. Instead of waiting for winter, Arthur, driven on by the militant anger of the Yorkshire miners, went into battle.

I sensed the mood earlier than anyone else. I was speaking at the Miner's Welfare Club at Cortonwood Colliery in South Yorkshire one Friday in 1984 when the bad news arrived that the colliery was to be closed. The hall filled with angry miners who clearly hadn't come to hear my carefully prepared speech on proportional representation. They had come to clamour for a strike and demanded to know what Labour was going to do about it. I hadn't the foggiest idea, but all I could manage to do then was waffle on about the importance of the coal industry and the effects of the over-valued pound.

The leader of the Labour Party, Neil Kinnock, didn't know what to do either. Support the strike or stand back? Arthur Scargill was absolutely clear what he had to do as National Union of Mineworkers president, and did what he'd been wanting to do for some time. He led the miners out on strike, convinced by their anger that there was no need for a ballot authorising their action. This was a conviction which undermined unity, because the Nottinghamshire miners, who had been the first to go back to work in the 1926 miners' strike, declined the call and mostly carried on working, leading to violent picketing of the Nottinghamshire pits.

The battle was long and hard. The full powers of the State were mobilised against this enemy within, turning the mining villages into battlegrounds. Police were drafted in from everywhere to maintain order and used like a military force, at times with cavalry, to break picket lines. Travel by those picketing was stopped, secret funds were channelled to the Nottinghamshire miners. Support funds coming to the NUM itself from Russia, Scandinavia and Libya were impounded, phones were tapped and an associate of Scargill suborned by the Secret Service to report on him. It was a disgraceful episode but one Margaret Thatcher won hands down. The miners were broken and beaten. They were forced back after a year. Immediate closures began. Except in Nottinghamshire.

By the mid-1980s Thatcher was triumphant. What her predecessor Harold Macmillan called the family silver had been sold off, too cheaply, but to great profitability, as the newly privatised entities fired workers and curtailed their social responsibilities. The stock exchange had been revivified by the "Big Bang" of getting rid of the gentlemanly restrictions which kept out the tough American banks and funds. These brought with them a greater appetite for risk and the practice, which British banks quickly learned, of speculating with the funds their customers had provided. The unions had been broken and chained down by law. The electorate was kept happy by cheap imports, easy credit and rising house prices, and Tory tenure was triumphantly renewed by yet another election victory in 1987. Every prospect seemed to please.

Except one. Neoliberalism is a philosophy best applied to economic management. So enthusiastic was the Thatcher government that it also took it into the more difficult areas of health and education reform, neither of them fields in which the market works effectively. In the health service, consortia of GPs became the purchasers of hospital services and inevitably were more generous to themselves than to the hospitals. This and underinvestment produced strains, longer waiting lists and pressure to go private, cutting right across the traditional close, co-operative relationships which kept the service going.

In education, the schools were given sums in cash and

expected to manage themselves and attract pupils by competition to produce better results, measured by actual achievement not value added. This in turn widened the gaps between schools with a better-off drawing area, which roared ahead, and those in poorer areas, whose problems were compounded. It also ran up against the opposition of the education unions and of parents. Yet the government persisted, and failed to learn the lesson that the market doesn't really work in either of these areas, but indeed can inflict positive damage. So the only answer is putting more money into both to alleviate the problems, not giving power to pushy parents and taking it from professional bodies which work best with co-operation and professional pride rather than market imperatives. Reform is no substitute for money.

In New Zealand by contrast, the imposition of the new regime began five years later and was more divisive and disruptive. Here the steamroller was driven not by the prime minister, David Lange, but by the finance minister, Roger Douglas. Douglas was a man who, like Thatcher, had got religion and an evangelical conviction that he was right; opponents were enemies, or probably mad, and had to be crushed by the roller for their own good. Normally the prime minister is all-powerful and the finance minister, however strong, is there to chart a policy acceptable to the boss. Things were different in New Zealand's fourth Labour government. An Auckland clique of Labour MPs – Douglas, Richard

Prebble, Mike Moore and Michael Bassett – had put Lange into power as leader and tended to think of him as their front man, there to entertain the crowd while they rebuilt the store. Lange didn't understand economics but enjoyed the impetus and éclat the new ideas gave his party. He was preoccupied with developing and later defending the policy of banning warships capable of carrying nuclear weapons, and selling it to a doubtful world.

The most eloquent, witty and impressive prime minister New Zealand ever had, Lange may well have had a sense of his own inadequacies, confessing early on to Margaret Pope, his speechwriter and eventual wife, "I don't think I can do this job". That diffidence revealed inner doubts, but it was wrong. Lange was brilliant at the presentational role. It was the political side he failed at. He could inspire audiences but was incapable of managing the party or handling the dirty nitty-gritty of politics and people management. He freely confessed his faults in his autobiography, *My Life*.

Most politicians write memoirs as "alibi-ographies" to prove how right they've been. Lange's, written when he knew his life was nearly over, is an honest description of his failings. He hated confrontation. He didn't have the people skills of managing a party and was incapable of the hard work of managing egos, building support, carrying colleagues, inform-ing the stupid and massaging enlarged egos. So he didn't bother. He didn't really like the party and the unions. When they began to protest at the impact of Rogernomics he neither listened to the malcontents nor gave them any leadership or support. He was brilliant at crisis management but created too many of the crises himself. His staff, though larger than Douglas's, showed neither the same fanatical dedication nor the same skills in handling the media. Douglas had the greater firepower as well as the fanatical adoration of new believers, such as the members of the Business Roundtable, or those who sought a Kiwi Thatcher to worship. He was better at managing the media than Lange with his joshing and jokes.

Colleagues report that though he was a good and efficient cabinet chair, Lange would arrive late or wander out and leave his ministers chuntering on. Because he was a quick reader and a fast decision-maker they assumed he was bored with their problems. The prime minister was really enjoying himself more than any prime minister should, loving the personal appearances, the speeches, the jousting with the press, the motor racing, the travel and his ability to inspire audiences. His aim was to improve the lot of the people; his plan was that Labour's first parliament would make the necessary reforms to revive the economy, then the second parliament would distribute the benefits with a new improved social security system, to be devised and developed by a Royal Commission under Sir Ivor Richardson, who was hauled out of the Privy Council in London and given an impossibly broad remit to plan it.

Lange was the amiable and likeable figurehead and the eloquent voice of the government, but the real driver of the programme was Douglas and his powerful finance team of Prebble and David Caygill. They ran the finance portfolio in a triumvirate, unlike Muldoon, who had run it on his own in combination with the prime ministership. They had come in to scrap Muldoon's authoritarianism and his methods but arrived without a manifesto to bind them. All they had was the compromise document drawn up, after stormy rows, by Deputy Prime Minister Geoffrey Palmer, who managed to produce a lawyer's cleverly ambiguous document capable of being interpreted several ways. Nor was the National Development Conference with which they started any real guide. Rather than building the corporate unity Lange had hoped for it merely allowed all the different sections to push their own barrows in their own directions.

The real programme was provided by Treasury's advice to the incoming government in 1984. The *Economic Management* document was a bold plan to liberalise the economy, open it up to the world and make all the market reforms Muldoon had refused to consider. This became Roger Douglas's agenda. Treasury had seized power and supplied a less than articulate finance minister with the programme, the arguments to justify it and the bumper slogans with which to put it across. Not being a great or a clear thinker, Douglas treated opposition with a superior "I know better" smirk but always had Treasury's words to offer when he did open his mouth. His own contribution was the drive and determination with which he implemented the programme they'd given him and which he now presented as his own. The drive was based on an iron conviction of his own rightness. People might not see it the same way as him but they would after the event. As he told the Mont Pelerin Society in Christchurch in 1989: "Consensus does not arise before quality decisions are made and implemented. It develops progressively after the decisions are implemented, as they deliver satisfactory outcomes to the public."

The programme therefore had to be delivered in major leaps by a kind of blitzkrieg which left opponents bemused. "Do not try to advance a step at a time," Douglas wrote later in his book *Unfinished Business*. "Define your objectives clearly and move towards them in quantum leaps. Otherwise the interest groups will have time to mobilise and drag you down." The clear inference was that in Britain Margaret Thatcher had been far too cautious and timid. The onslaught would bring its own rewards by turning the vested interests against each other. "After you remove its privileges and make plain that the clock cannot be turned back, the group starts to focus on removing the privileges of other groups that still hold up its own costs." Then and only then do "people begin to grasp the idea that wherever a group manages to hold on to privilege and protection, an avoidable cost is imposed on those who are learning to adjust". Turn each against the other and the reformer has won without the messy procedures, debate and delay of democracy.

Impetus was all. Douglas had it and the process was so powerful and quick that it precluded thought and discussion and gave opponents neither the time nor the opportunity to make a stand. There wasn't even time to discuss it. Why waste time on yammering when Roger knew what was right?

Douglas drove the steamroller, Treasury supplied the map and the Business Roundtable of New Zealand's top executives provided the fuel. They gained increasing influence over the driver as time passed, inflating his egotistical determination, supplying the advice and fuel additives and encouraging the driver on to the wilder shores of economic liberalism where their own interest lay.

It was dynamic, exciting and, for a time, successful. Subsidies and support for farming were removed, hitting small towns and rural areas. Then, to ensure equal treatment, the import controls were removed from manufacturing. New Zealand was to be exposed to a cold, competitive world. The dollar was floated and promptly went up because the monetarist parts of the programme made interest rates far too high, which brought money flooding in. Apparently, the cost of everything was to be cut but not that of money. Competition brought change and Douglas congratulated himself loudly about the benefits to air travel from bringing Ansett in to compete with the national carrier in 1987, until

Ansett New Zealand went bust in 2000 and packed its services in.

Government departments and agencies were turned into State Owned Enterprises committed to making a profit, though the government claimed, Scout's honour, that it had no intention of selling them. Competition was encouraged but where it couldn't develop, because New Zealand was too small, everything should be contestable in order that rivals could come in if the incumbent became too powerful.

The decisions of Douglas and his team were accepted by cabinet committees which they dominated and which in turn assured them of passage in cabinet with a few demurrals. The Labour Party Caucus, which I'd always praised as giving New Zealand MPs a real influence in contrast to our bigger and more amorphous British Parliamentary Labour Party, proved unable to resist, because cabinet and its acolytes voted as a bloc under collective responsibility and carried the day. The business community and Business Roundtable urged them on, and sang Roger's praises. Some members even began to contribute to him and the party. It was euphoric. The only real dissent came from the Left and the unions. It was disregarded or dismissed as Luddism. Lange declined to listen.

Awash with approbation and money from business, Labour won the 1987 election triumphantly. Its vote went up, though the core vote in safe electorates dropped away. New Zealand was the poster boy of the new economics, a world leader in liberalisation and free-market reform. And then the game changed. After the election in October 1987, the New Zealand stock market crashed. Shares lost 20 percent of their value in one day. Company frauds and fiddles were revealed and several dodgy companies went under, taking people's savings with them and reducing several reputations from hero to zero. As American billionaire and philanthropist Warren Buffett remarked, "You only find out who is swimming naked when the tide goes out". Several of New Zealand's new elite were.

David Lange, who had been growing uneasy about the pace and the nature of Douglas's reforms, now, belatedly, put his foot down. He was increasingly concerned by the over-optimistic scenarios he was getting from Roger and resented the efforts Roger and his team were making to obstruct and undermine his cherished Royal Commission on Welfare, to which he was looking to develop plans to distribute to the people the growth and revenues which Rogernomics was supposed to provide. First the pain. Then the gain. Except that the gain became a mirage. Lange took advice from critics, saw the growing distress, and periodically sent Helen Sutch (daughter of Bill Sutch), down to Balclutha to report on the findings of the freezing works manager who had been recording the effects and the local impact of the reforms.

Lange's speech writer, Margaret Pope, who had by this

time become his mistress, put ideological lead in his pencil. She saw more clearly than he where Roger Douglas's reforms led and the damage they were doing to Labour's people. By the end of 1987 the fun prime minister had become deadly serious and ready to act. His chance came when Douglas and the triumvirate seized the opportunity of the crash to unveil a single tax plan which they claimed would cure the problem. This was to be accompanied by an increase in Douglas's regressive GST, to be used to compensate low earners whose tax was increased by the new system. These plans were already being developed when the financial crash provided the excuse to introduce them.

Instead of adopting a Keynesian solution and boosting spending as a stimulus Roger Douglas saw a revolutionary shift in the balance of taxation away from wealth as the way to restore confidence. A paper drafted in his office called for a quantum leap forward, and said that a package was the only way to balance out the pluses and minuses, in order to make them acceptable. The cabinet agreed, hesitantly and tentatively, to a single tax rate which benefitted the wealthy, penalised the poor, reduced state revenues and would have the effect of forcing the State to curtail spending and welfare. It was cushioned by income support but, as Lange pointed out to his finance minister, that could always be withdrawn by a Tory government, while the reduction in revenue was unacceptable because it would require further spending cuts to restore the balance and finance the work of his Royal Commission.

So, with Roger out of the country, Lange scrapped it unilaterally. While the caucus was still discussing the issue, Lange walked out, called a press conference and announced the single-rate tax package had been cancelled. (A two-tier option was later introduced.) This precipitated civil war. Prime minster and finance minister denounced each other in published letters. Richard Prebble was moved out of Treasury to State Owned Enterprises and 18 of them, including Telecom (which Labour's manifesto had promised to keep), were sold off in an "everything must go" fire sale to reduce the growing public debt. The *New Zealand Herald*'s satirical poet Whim Wham wrote: "Tell Richard not to sell Mount Cook, / But Stewart Island's worth a Look."

Everything went at knock-down prices to pay off debt, but at the cost of enormous fees to those who brokered the sales. The new bodies then cut labour forces to boost profits. The Forestry Service became the Forest Corporation of New Zealand and then Forest Corp. Sixty percent of its workforce was laid off, all of them leaving with the assurance that the job they had taken pride in hadn't been worth doing and they should be grateful for the opportunity to find real work. The Royal Commission now served no real purpose. Roger Douglas's reforms and the new tax structures meant that there was no money to improve the system. Sir Ivor

Richardson gave up, chucked several fat volumes of evidence but no proposals onto the market, and left, muttering angrily. Lange's fig leaf was snatched away.

This began an endgame, which turned into political farce. The rebels formed a ginger group, called the Backbone Club, and denounced Lange up and down the country as certifiably insane. Roger Douglas resigned. Caucus reinstated him when another vacancy came up. Lange, censured for announcing New Zealand's withdrawal from the Southeast Asia Treaty Organisation without cabinet authorisation, resigned. Geoffrey Palmer became a reluctant (and transient) prime minister in 1989, with David Caygill as his finance minister. Roger's Revolution was over. The financial and commercial interests which had backed it and supported it in the 1987 election transferred their affections and, more importantly, their money to the National Party, which won the 1990 election with ease.

As Rogernomics ended in the land of the rising dollar the same discontents were coming to the fore in Britain because of Margaret Thatcher's policies in the land of the rising pound. Being too long in the job brings hubris. It makes prime ministers messianic, inclined to believe in their own infallibility. As Thatcher was afflicted by both conditions she surrounded herself misguidedly with courtiers and got rid of her critics. Nigel Lawson, her reforming chancellor, resigned in 1989 in protest at the influence of Alan Walters, her adviser. She drove Michael Heseltine to resign, fired Geoffrey Howe, her loyal servant, and over-reached herself with the imposition of a poll tax, the first in England since the 14th century. The poll tax, officially called the Community Charge, was introduced in Scotland in 1989 and England and Wales the following year. It was designed to ensure that everyone paid the costs of local government, not just property owners, a principle which pleased Thatcher. But when it turned out not to be the anticipated £70 or so per head but £300, millions had to be taken to court for debt and serious riots broke out in London. A good idea became a looming disaster.

When Thatcher added an attempt to extend her liberalisation programme to a battle with the European Economic Community, euro-enthusiasts took up arms, Geoffrey Howe denounced her rather quaintly for not playing cricket, and she was forced into an unwanted leadership election in 1990. When, thanks to incompetent campaigning and her own proud refusal to stoop to electioneering, she failed to win by a big enough majority, she was forced to resign in tears. The Conservative Party elected the more emollient John Major. He cancelled the poll tax, stopped the rush of reforms and ended the war with Europe by signing the Maastricht Treaty in 1992, which his fellow ministers declared as a victory for him, game, set and match.

Thus, in Britain the neoliberal revolution ground to a halt because its first evangelist, Margaret Thatcher, was

ignominiously thrown out. At this point, in Britain and
New Zealand, the process of building worlds fit for Milton
Friedman to live in diverged. In Britain it came to a halt.
The damage done was concealed by North Sea oil, which
paid the nation's way in the world, as Britain's shrinking
manufacturing industry could no longer do. Oil compensated
the government for its loss of revenues by its tax flows and
kept the electorate happy by financing the imports the new
consumer society craved. In New Zealand, on the other hand,
the march down Dead-End Street continued at an even
faster pace. Labour had left the structures and the finances
for social security intact. The incoming National government now launched an attack on them, on the trade unions
and on health, as well as imposing more neoliberal cuts
and reforms.

Neoliberalism came more naturally, though later, to New
Zealand's conservative National Party. National endorsed the
new religion as soon as they had got rid of the embarrassment
of Rob Muldoon, a long, painful and ultimately sad process,
given his inability to stop back-seat driving and the sadness
of his leaving-party from parliament in 1991, when none of
the ministers he'd bullied turned up. Jim Bolger, the new
prime minister, under pressure from the Business Roundtable,
appointed Ruth Richardson, a miniature Thatcher and a
passionate liberaliser, as minister of finance. Ruthenomics
replaced Douglas's Rogernomics.

National had won the 1990 election on hopes of a rest from remorseless radicalism. It promised to create a "decent society", which the electorate interpreted as the return to normal they wanted. They didn't get it. Ruth, using the excuse of a deficit left by Labour, began a three-front war on what remained of the social democratic society. The 1991 Mother of All Budgets (as Ruth herself called it) increased GST and cut benefits. The minimum wage was reduced, the Bank of New Zealand sold to Australia and student loans were introduced to finance higher education. The arbitration system was scrapped and replaced by individual contracts, which effectively castrated the trade unions.

National also repeated the Thatcherite mistake of pushing the market into the health service in the hope of saving money on the growing health bill. In a fatal Friedmanite flourish the health service was commercialised by a purchaser-provider split recommended by a hospitals taskforce headed by Alan Gibbs, which Labour had appointed but wisely not implemented. The approach was far more drastic and abrupt than Thatcher's in Britain and because it was compounded by underinvestment in the service the hostility it produced was greater. Hospitals became Crown Health Enterprises, run by businessmen. The consequences ranged from disastrous to comic, and were portrayed by Ian Cowan, a radiologist at Christchurch Hospital, in his novel *Not Our Problem* which offers a hilarious indictment through exaggeration, including proposals to paint the whole hospital peach and rename wards to make them less forbidding ("Stitch in Time" for the operating theatre, "Take a Break" for the fracture ward), but in reality money was wasted on commissioning expensive logos and letterheads, hiring consultants and on employing lawyers to draw up the thousands of contracts which now became necessary.

By its humour the book brings out the real-world follies of commercialisation, as new executives set out overconfidently to reach a precisely estimated target for economies created by consultants without knowing how the estimates had been arrived at. Managers multiplied, money was channelled to accountants, consultants, lawyers and public relations people and wasted on expensive logos while beds and medical staff were cut and services reduced. The new men understood neither the co-operative ethos of the health service nor the responsibilities of doctors who weren't workers on an assembly line.

A character in Cowan's novel echoes the conclusion drawn by the real head of the Health Funding Agency, Graham Scott, formerly head of Treasury, who said: "The reason that the expected savings were not realised when the market was reformed was that the doctors just kept on treating patients and that was not what they were supposed to do in response to the signals which were being sent."

Jim Bolger, a much shrewder figure than Lange, removed

Health Minister Simon Upton and took the opportunity to move Ruth Richardson after the 1993 election. She sulked, resigned and went off to exile on her farm, a Canterbury St Helena, where a University of Canterbury student, Andrew Dean, later interviewed her. He was angered by the student loans. Richardson was charming but absolutely unrepentant, extolling the virtues of creative destruction and telling Dean, "your words of discomfort, loss and disconnection don't resonate with me at all".

Thus, neoliberalism had led to three parties being thrown out of office, the ejection of three prime ministers and six finance ministers, and alienated electors who'd never been consulted in the first place. Quite a track record, to which one has to add the higher unemployment, the bankruptcies and the decline of manufacturing in both countries. Yet none of the perpetrators apologised for any of it. Margaret Thatcher believed she had been right to the end. Any failures were due to the weakness and inadequacies of others. The other leading advocates, Nigel Lawson, Geoffrey Howe, Nicholas Ridley, Keith Joseph, admitted no mistakes; what they'd done had to be done and they earned the usual British politicians' pension by writing alibi-ographies to prove it.

In New Zealand, the reaction of the perpetrators diverged. Geoffrey Palmer, Labour's reluctant prime minister, when he looked back at all Labour's economic measures in his memoir *Reform*, said, "I cannot see any of the measures in the list

[…] that with the wisdom of hindsight I would change, with the exception of privatisation. And I would change that not because it was a bad way to reduce the debt but because it was massively unpopular." Roger and Ruth both continued to argue that their work was incomplete. One more heave would bring them to the promised land, which was the theme of Roger's later book, *Unfinished Business*.

Others admitted that the revolution might not have totally succeeded but was still right and inevitable, rather like one of those evangelists who preach the end of the world then, when it doesn't happen, tell their congregation that it has but no one's noticed. Alan Gibbs, a founding member of the Act Party, had transferred his allegiance seamlessly from Roger to Ruth and claimed benefits which would have come anyway. In a TVNZ documentary in 1996, he judged New Zealand after the revolution to be "an extremely exciting place", declaring, "There is nothing you can't do in New Zealand that you could do anywhere else. The communications are rapid, you're plugged into the world not just in terms of talking to people but in terms of exchanging services with them. People with enterprise in New Zealand can now undertake activities that would have been impossible in the old economy…" Nonetheless, he left for England in 1997 to pursue his amphibian car project.

Several other big movers – Sir Michael Fay, David Richwhite, Douglas Myers, Ron Brierley – also left the country. Leading politicians became consultants, selling advice to the rest of the world to tell them how to get themselves into the same mess as New Zealand. Roger Douglas was particularly voluble and persuaded both major parties in Australia to damage themselves by introducing GST. Graham Scott had to be happy advising Mongolia, which junked his reforms shortly afterwards.

Only David Lange showed any contrition. Making a sad farewell speech to the House of Representatives in 1996, he argued that there was good and bad in his government's record, "but the balance of history will be that it was for the good". He went on: "I want to thank all those people who were wrecked by us. They had been taught for years that they had the right to an endless treadmill of prosperity and assurance and we did them. People over 60 hate me. They hate me because I was the symbol of what caused that assurance of support and security to be shattered. That is something that has always been part of my burden."

The electorate was tired of remorseless change, which achieved so little at the cost of so much pain. New Zealand's GDP fell by 0.7 percent, the worst record of any advanced country, unemployment doubled and cradle-to-grave welfare was scrapped. The people no longer believed claims that the pain was worth the gain because the result was all pain for no gain. They wanted a rest. As Lange had put it, it was "time for a cup of tea". People turned to the traditional provider of tea

71

and cake, the Labour Party, which was now promising a fairer, fresher approach in Britain, and returning to its former role and principles in New Zealand. The march down Dead-End Street was halted. Temporarily.

CHAPTER FIVE

TIME FOR A BREAK

AFTER A DECADE AND MORE of religious rapture – from 1979 to 1992 in Britain, and 1984 to 1994 in New Zealand – the crusade was halted. The post-war settlement of growth, full employment and welfare had been knocked down. Demolition had begun on the benign state, which since World War II had been insulating, protecting, regulating and managing for growth. A new generation of market-minded politicians had taken over, inspired by Friedrich Hayek, Ayn Rand and Milton Friedman rather than John Maynard Keynes. They were all dedicated to pushing the balances back and opening up the two economies.

It had been an exciting but exhausting demolition job that left the parties divided and squabbling. Their electors were fed up with remorseless change, which they had neither asked for nor expected, and which wasn't delivering the benefits claimed for it. People were tired of governments which promised to put things right but immediately began to pull up everything by the roots and put it back again, usually upside down. Even those preaching the new religion wanted a rest.

The hubble, bubble, toil and trouble of the revolution had upset the stabilities of the long conservative tenure of power in the affluent years. Now the electorate was throwing out governments more frequently, minor parties multiplied in New Zealand, and in England the third party, the Liberals, began to grow. The two countries' conservative parties pulled back to the centre ground of moderate, compassionate conservatism, as conservative parties usually do. In New Zealand, Jim Bolger's National Party government pulled back only after three more years of creative destruction and then a near-defeat in the 1993 election. This forced Bolger into a coalition with Winston Peters, the former National MP whose New Zealand First party won 17 seats in 1996, the first general election under proportional representation. Peters had to be made deputy prime minister to keep National in power. This made Bolger turn to moderation. Neither National in New Zealand, nor the Conservative Party in Britain was happy with their respective retreats to the centre because both had been doing, in their neoliberal phase, things that they'd always wanted to do but which had not been politically possible in the Keynesian era. Now both saw sense in an enforced rest. This would please the people and allow the politicians to draw breath, however many grumbles it produced within their parties.

Labour's electors in both countries had suffered more damage in terms of loss of jobs, benefits and union power, so

Labour had a more difficult task of revision and reform. Now both Labour parties behaved in their traditional fashion and fell apart. Both began internal fights which amounted to civil war. The argument in Britain was whether the party should move Left to appeal to a resurgent proletarian vote radicalised by Thatcherism, or whether it should move right to recruit more satisfied southern and middle-class electors to its basic working-class support. In New Zealand, the argument was whether the party should return to its old basic role as protector of the working class and abandon its flirtation with finance and neoliberalism, or whether it should be proud of what it had done and continue on the same path. In both parties the moderates won, though they took far longer in Britain than in a New Zealand Labour Party more accustomed to quick re-sprays and sudden changes in its more vacuous philosophy.

The first stage of Labour's weaning process was presided over by Mike Moore, the New Zealand Labour Party's third leader in just over a year, who became prime minister for a few months in 1990 and led the party in opposition until 1993. He began to return the party to its old corporate system of working with the unions and improved both votes and numbers in the 1993 election. Then, having failed in two successive elections, a party which had made leadership changes a system of management replaced him with Helen Clark, a woman of firmer principles who had kept her head down in the Lange government. As leader from December 1993, she dedicated herself, in partnership with Michael Cullen, a more vocal dissenter in the Douglas era, to pulling the party together and taking it back to its old welfare programme.

A party without a clear and strong ideology such as the New Zealand Labour Party had been easily taken over in the 1980s. Now it reverted with similar ease to its old norms. Pressure to do so was increased by a party split of the type which had happened in Britain in 1981, when the Social Democrat Party broke away from Labour. That split had been to the Right of a Left-wing party; in New Zealand, the split was to the Left of a Labour Party which was pursuing radically Right-wing policies. Jim Anderton, a one-man opposition in the Lange government, left the Labour Party, and retained his seat as New Labour. In 1991, he had formed and led the Alliance Party, bringing together disgruntled Labour people, Greens, Democrats, a Maori party and a few nationalists. In 1993, the last general election under the first-past-the-post system, this Alliance of the disgruntled won 18 percent of the vote and two seats. This created a prospect not only of doing better when proportional representation came in to boost minor parties, but of exerting more effective pressure on the Labour Party from outside than had ever been possible for the Left working within the party, where it was usually discounted and disregarded.

Had Labour won the 1993 election, this would have been a powerful role. Labour didn't. Nor did it win in 1996. By the next election in 1999, which Labour did win, the Alliance was down to 8 percent of the vote and 10 seats under the Mixed Member Proportional (MMP) voting system. At this point Anderton chose the path of power, joining the government as deputy prime minister rather than pushing it from the outside as a pressure group. A reformed Labour government under Helen Clark took power and the Alliance effectively broke up, falling to a mere 1.3 percent of the vote in the 2002 election. In the eyes of critics like academic and Alliance candidate Jim Flynn and Alliance organiser Matt McCarten, ego had thrown away opportunity. Anderton argued that the Alliance had done its work by pulling Labour back to Labour ground and purging it of Rogernomics. Both were correct, but as usual in New Zealand politics, practicality triumphed over ideals.

In Britain, Labour's travails were harder and its exile from power longer, 18 years to be exact. Neil Kinnock took over as leader in 1983 and began to jettison the huge list of promises in the party's manifesto of that year, described as "the longest suicide note in history". He dumped the party's two biggest albatrosses: nuclear disarmament and withdrawal from the European Common Market. The Labour Party conference regularly supported nuclear disarmament, but Labour governments had never implemented it; withdrawal from the Common Market had been in the 1983 manifesto but was blithely ignored by the Right of the party. Kinnock stood on his head on both issues and persuaded the party to do the same.

Then, after a brief period of leadership by John Smith, a popular mainstream figure who died in 1994, Tony Blair was elected leader. He was a much more attractive leader, though less eloquent than Kinnock. He added another dead albatross to Labour's slaughter of butchered birds by dropping Clause Four of Labour's constitution, with its promise of the public ownership of the means of production, distribution and exchange. This included, opponents claimed, every corner shop and hairdresser, but it was a symbolic non-issue, daft, and as relevant to the modern party as the 16th-century Thirty-nine Articles were to the Church of England. Labour governments had done nothing about Clause Four, but, Blairites claimed, it frightened people. Getting rid of it would show that the party was New Labour, a nicer, gentler and safer party, eminently electable. It also showed Blair as a new modernising presence. After a brief struggle the traditionalists were beaten and the clause changed, because, as I commented at the time, "If the leader jumps off a cliff the party has no alternative but to follow him." The clause change was merely symbolic, but clever public relations, and in 1997 Labour was overwhelmingly elected, helped by the fact that the Tories were falling apart over Europe.

Opponents make much of the fact that Blair, like the Liberal Democrats' leader later on, Nick Clegg, was one of those bright, personable, upper-class kids who could really belong to any party. The accusation is true, and Blair had hesitated and considered whether he should join Labour, like his wife, or the Tories, like his father. But once in, his barrister skills of arguing any case were enormously beneficial for Labour. Blair was an idealist. He believed strongly in education, tackling child poverty and deprivation and giving people less well off than himself a fair deal. He wasn't a socialist and saw public ownership as unnecessary, but he saw that both socialism and the framework of controls and management which had given Britain the affluent years were too difficult and contentious to be possible in the age of globalisation. So, in his view, the concerns of the Labour Party should now be welfare and betterment for the mass of the people; a fair society but not the equal society Tony Crosland had urged in *The Future of Socialism* in 1956.

The new leader had no ideology, merely a vague mishmash of beliefs collectively described as the Third Way. This included a "reinvention" of government ruled by the "rigour" of the market. This worried me at the time because it indicated that the market not the State was in control. There would also be "pre-distribution" through better support services, and an increase in equality. The last would be achieved through a minimum wage and tax credits, to boost low pay, and much improved public provision in education and health, both of which had been badly hit by substantial underinvestment in the Tory years. No word of socialism, public ownership, controls or trade union power, and no proposals to reverse the damage done by the Conservative Party or to renationalise the family silver Thatcher had sold off. Here, critics said, was a son of Thatcher, and his credentials became clear when the first act of the new government was to make the Bank of England independent and give up government's powers to control interest rates. Labour's first act in 1945 had been to nationalise the Bank of England. Now in 1997 its first was to privatise it.

This suited the mood of the moment. No drastic change. No ideology. Elements of Thatcherism but with a smiling friendly face, a skill in which Blair specialised. It made the party respectable, allayed fear and was sold with enthusiasm by a party which now offered itself as a consumer good with a powerful sales department. Labour was as safe as a neutered Pekinese under Blair and, unlike the domineering Boadicea of the Tory party, it was people- and business-friendly.

Blair's chancellor of the exchequer was Gordon Brown, another son of Thatcher, who believed, as she and Blair both did, in the free market, globalisation, deregulation and lower taxes. Blair and Brown made a great double act; the smiling, thespian leader and the dour iron chancellor. Like so many double acts, they were also rivals who came over the years to hate each other, with Brown thinking that his leader had agreed to go once Labour was established as a party of government. Blair, loving the job and donning the messianic mantle, became reluctant to give it up easily or soon.

The initial impact of their partnership was an enormous

success. The poor were protected by minimum wages, by tax credits, by housing benefits to subsidise rents and by hundreds of Sure Start children's centres to provide pre-schooling for children, and health, cooking and education classes for mothers. Money poured into health and education but not into housing, because the government estimated the cost of new building and refurbishment of the council stock at £19 billion. This the new government couldn't spend without raising taxes, so it continued the Thatcher sales and bribed, bluffed and bullied councils into transferring their stock to housing associations to raise the money on the private market. This in turn meant that the provision of public housing for rent became less and less adequate as the stock reduced, because the Tory policy of "right to buy" at a big discount was maintained, and new build figures fell to 1920 levels.

All this couldn't be paid for without much more government borrowing and spending than Labour wanted, so the government turned to the private sector to finance schools, hospitals, roads and facilities by Private Finance Initiative (PFI) contracts. Under PFIs, the private sector built, owned and serviced the buildings and could, initially, sell the completed contract on at a profit. This was a more expensive way of doing things. It kept the public sector borrowing figures down, but it led to real financial strain for several hospitals. In the case of London Underground development, it also led to the collapse and liquidation of two companies doing the job and considerable expenditure by government to have the work completed.

Nevertheless, the government continued undeterred. Even the Treasury building in Whitehall was privatised to a company in Jamaica. When I did a period of parliamentary service with the Royal Navy, I found that the fisheries protection vessels were all privately owned and rented to the government, as were the aircraft used for mock attacks in naval exercises. The attack hours were carefully restricted to guarantee a profit to the owners. My suggestion that the navy change its song to 'Rent Britannia' was not taken seriously. Rather than getting out and competing in world markets, British capitalism was leeching off the State. Consultants sold the idea to other countries, none of whom embarked on it as enthusiastically (or as expensively) as the British, but then their capitalism was more prone to build up the strength of their states, not bleed it.

Not every prospect pleased. Manufacturing continued to shrink and the pound was complacently allowed to rise to levels that were far too high. This penalised exports. So the trade deficit grew. Yet some prospects certainly did please. The economy grew at 3 percent with the huge stimulus inherited from the devaluation of the pound forced on the Tories in 1992. This had occurred when Britain was forced out of the European Exchange Rate Mechanism, and because consumer spending, much of it now financed by borrowing, increased. House prices rose, making incumbents feel better off; health and education improved. Gordon Brown began to assume that he had found a new paradigm of economic management which would provide continuous growth and eliminate boom and bust. Self-congratulation carried on into the new century. Labour was what Blair had wanted it to be: a successful party of government relegating the Conservatives to the futility of opposition. Permanently, he hoped.

Hubris comes before a fall and as Labour's was greater than the Tories' had been, so was its fall. First came Blair's wars, when he played Robin to George W. Bush's Batman by sending troops to ill-considered wars in Afghanistan in 2001 and Iraq in 2003. These produced massive protests and the performance of British troops in Basra and Helmand was so poor that in both they had to be rescued by the Americans. The British electorate quite likes wars, but prefers them to be short and victorious. These weren't.

However, the wars were not so much the problem as Gordon Brown. He finally succeeded, after a long period of attrition, in pushing Blair out in 2007, only to prove a clumsy and inept prime minister, more Mr Bean than Master Wonderful. He was also an indecisive manager, too frightened to seize his opportunity of a general election to validate a new government, and abandoning his carefully cultivated Left-wing image to fawn on Finance and pander to the City of London. Everything Finance wanted it got, so that funny money, dodgy funds, Arab sheikhs, drug barons and Russian oligarchs poured into Taxhaven-on-Thames, pushing the pound, and London property prices, ever higher as they seized the opportunities created by the fact that Britannia now waived the rules rather than ruled the waves. No one thought that what flowed in so easily and massively could now flow out just as easily.

This was neither a new paradigm nor the economic miracle Gordon claimed (and, even worse, genuinely believed) it was. Finance was blowing up a huge bubble, inflated by ever-rising property and asset prices and ever-greater risks. Following my old pattern of writing to Britain's chancellors to tell them (free of charge) how to do their job, I wrote several times to tell Gordon about the old and very basic economic law "If a thing can't go on forever, it probably won't". Gordon never replied. He always got his junior ministers to do that, in letters which indicated that they hadn't a high enough IQ to understand the issue. Ed Balls, the man closest to Gordon, explains that Gordon "tended to hand over only the issues he didn't care so much about or, on occasion, didn't want to touch with a bargepole". Had I realised that, I'd have known much more quickly where I stood – a mere galley slave on the ship of state.

Nor was it much use speaking out. Politicians had been deeply discredited by *The Daily Telegraph*'s 2009 disclosure of the ludicrous expenses claims by MPs for moats, duck houses, gardening, wisteria, booze and even a little light pornography. We were all discredited by the greed of a few. Respect collapsed, abuse piled up and faeces dropped through letter boxes as people came to believe that MPs were a pack of greedy spongers all out for themselves and certainly not a reliable source of opinions and advice. When I published my warnings about the coming crash the only response was a series of invitations to push them down the lavatory I'd had repainted at public expense.

Meanwhile, New Zealand Labour was embarked on the same ameliorative programme as the British party. It didn't have the glamour of Tony Blair but it had honest, reliable Helen Clark, who was a much tougher and more experienced leader, with a firmer ideology. In 1999 she came to power without the overwhelming majority Blair had secured two years before but sustained by deals with the Alliance, the everlasting Peter Dunne (three decades in parliament and after 2008 the sole MP for his United Future party) and New Zealand First, whose leader, Winston Peters, became an almost-but-never-quite Labour man and an excellent foreign minister.

As in Britain the programme was improvement not reversal. The effort to financialise health and education was dropped and both got more government investment to repair the damage. Those hardest hit by market economics got increases in the minimum wage, a halt to the process of raising state house rents to market levels and an end to interest on student loans during study. Working for Families provided tax credits for those in work, then airways and railways were taken back into public ownership and Kiwibank was set up, at the Alliance's insistence, to use the facilities of New Zealand Post to compete with the big Australian banks. KiwiSaver came in to boost retirement savings.

All told, it was a solid rather than spectacular record but it made life better for most people. It was stronger and more radical than Blair's, and Clark had the good sense to send medics and engineers rather than front-line combat troops to Iraq, despite strong American pressure. Better terms of trade and the growth of the Chinese market both boosted economic growth and employment. As Labour's party political broad-casts put it, things were getting better. But not fast enough, and the gains were received with an amazing ingratitude by a petty and fractious opposition and an anti-feminist media obsessed with creating an image of a bossy matron of a prime pinister who favoured Maori and women but bullied poor hapless, vulnerable men.

In both countries, the pause for a rest and a cup of tea had brought a successful halt to remorseless liberalisation, but no reversal. It provided a chance to remedy some of the deficien-cies and failures of the market and to improve the lot of those who had suffered most from the excesses of the previous period. It had shifted the Left from socialism, controls and political structures to welfare and fairness. However, it had neither provided a new alternative ideology, nor reduced the excessive power of Finance by shifting effort and investment back to production. Nor did it develop the structures and regulations which would protect the two nations from the excesses and dangers of the huge money flows to which the world was being exposed. Neither government had, in fact, thought much of even considering such protections, let alone creating them. Their nervous commitment to respectability and to being business-friendly precluded restraints on the new paradigm, and the efforts in parliamentary committees to consider new regulations on New Zealand's Wild West financial sector were pushed aside.

Which was a tragic failure. In 2008, the pause for tea abruptly ended. The Great Recession, itself the direct consequence of the massive speculative money flows, hit the US and spread out from there to the rest of the world. That which couldn't go on forever had come shuddering to a painful and unexpected stop.

CHAPTER SIX
THE GREAT RECESSION

WITH THE BREAK-UP OF the post-war settlement, effectively begun by the "Nixon Shock" of 1971, America went off gold, exchange rates floated to convertibility and currencies became less stable. Inflation led to high interest rates and a rising pound and dollar. Controls were abandoned, the restraints on Finance introduced after the Crash of 1929 were eased and in some cases abolished, as was the Glass-Steagall Act in America, which had stopped banks speculating with customers' money. At the behest of Wall Street it was scrapped by Bill Clinton in 1999. The separation between the two arms of banks was also scrapped in Britain by the "Big Bang" deregulation of 1986, abolishing the gentlemanly intermediaries on the stock exchange to attract the American big banks to play there. Just as American tennis stars loved to play (and beat the Brits) at Wimbledon.

Rock-solid mutuals like insurance companies and building societies, financed by the subscriptions of members, were turned into limited companies or banks and began to raise huge sums on money markets to take on more risk to make more profit. The big four accountancy houses, frightened of lawsuits if their audits failed in the world of fast speculation and creative accountancy, won limited liability status to protect the houses and yachts of their partners by buying (and writing) protective legislation in Jersey, then threatening to move there. The British government gave in and legislated for Limited Liability Partnerships (LLPs), thus giving cover to fraudsters as well as the dark-suited mafia of accountancy.

All this facilitated the rise of Finance; caged since the 1930s, set free in the 1980s and growing in power, indeed dominance, in Britain, where the City had always been excessively strong. Banks became international, funds and neo-banks became ever more important and financiers became, in Tom Wolfe's world, the new Masters of the Universe, lords of all they surveyed. Or owned or speculated on.

Which meant growing risk. Production and manufacturing, both encouraged by the post-war settlement, are stable forces boosting productivity and producing investment, employment and economic growth, working best in a stable environment. Finance is by its nature unstable. It is driven by risk, gains by speculation, and profits from uncertainty. Manufacturing builds on steady investment and co-operation within the firm. Finance acts in a herd and works in a frenzy. Production thinks and builds long-term. Finance's priorities are short-term, speculative and greedy.

Deregulation provided the opportunity for excess, but the rising tide of money provided the dynamic. A world awash with money, where Finance was enthroned, debt growing exponentially and speculation rife, was clearly stumbling towards some kind of crash. A series of warning tremors, particularly in the US, foretold of the dangers. They included the Savings and Loan scandal of the late 1970s and 1980s, which saw the failure of more than 1000 savings and loan associations; the crash of Long-Term Capital Management, a gigantic hedge fund, in the 1990s; the Asian Financial Crisis; the Enron crash in 2001. There were assorted frauds and insolvencies in New Zealand's version of the Wild Financial West: Judge Corp, Equitycorp, other corpses like Feltex, and a series of investment funds which were basically Ponzi schemes paying out as dividends the money coming in for investment.

The laxity of regulation became clear to me when I got proof that foreign exchange dealers were robbing their customers by taking a few points off transactions for themselves or the treasury of the bank. This was an easy thing to do now daily foreign exchange transactions went into billions, a far higher figure than was needed to finance world trade. Minute-by-minute price fluctuations made it easy to take the best rate for themselves and quote the worst to the client. I raised the issue in parliament and took the evidence to the Bank of England. No one wanted to know, though 20 years later I was proved right by lawsuits in the US where trading was exactly the same as in Britain. A few points a day and dealers, regarded as the barrow boys of Finance, made a rich living. They still do. The authorities want to indulge not discipline them. So they refused to provide the simple protection I suggested of requiring time stamps on all transactions.

Rising to the new opportunities, banks, and Finance, expanded, went international and poured out credit on an unprecedented scale. Reserve requirements, originally set at 20 percent of lending, were progressively reduced to 3 percent in the UK. Their balance sheets grew from 200 percent of GDP in the 1980s to 500 percent by 2007. The gross debt of the whole financial system rose to two and a half times the world's total GDP, creating enormous competition to lend which took banks well beyond safe limits. Iceland's three banks, Landsbanki, Kaupthing and Glitnir, created credit 10 times greater than their tiny nation's GDP to finance increasingly risky investments by Icelandic millionaires buying everything that moved (and a lot that didn't, like West Ham United Football Club). They raised money to lend by paying higher interest to British investors. The Irish banks were much the same but with a whiff of corruption.

New inventions boosted the speculation even further. One was derivative trading, not in commodities but in their future prices, a form of gambling (on which no gambling tax was paid) which was boosted further by leverage. This was borrowing to make still bigger bets, producing a higher return but a greater risk if the bet didn't come off. Another innovation was Collateralised Debt Obligations (CDOs), which allowed lenders to package debts, good, bad and hopeless, and have them securitised, insured and rated, usually highly, by the rating agencies which drew fees for the process. CDOs conferred the ability to make ever-more risky loans because the buyers of the debt knew nothing of the borrowers. They also brought a return to the lender, allowing it to make still more loans.

In many cases the top executives of banks didn't even seem to know what their underlings were doing. Michael Lewis reveals this in his book *The Big Short*, about the Global Financial Crisis of 2007–2008, now a film, which shows how a small group of idealists tried to warn the banks, then, when the banks took no notice, decided to bet against the trend. Alistair Darling, a British chancellor of the exchequer, bears this out, saying of the top bank management: "They didn't understand what they were doing, the risks they were taking on, or, often, the products they were selling ... The top management in banks both here and in the US, failed to understand – or even ask – what was apparently making them so much profit and what were the risks." To which one might add, why should they? They were getting bonuses from the profits and had no personal liability for any failure.

Risk piled on risk in a system awash with money, much

of it coming from international imbalances. Under the old gold standard before World War I, imbalances were self-correcting. A nation trading at a surplus drew in gold, which boosted inflation and increased costs, thus making its exports less attractive and checking the inflow. With fixed exchange rates, on the other hand, nations became successful by keeping their exchange rates down. This meant developing economies like Germany, Japan and later Korea, Taiwan and ultimately China could build up powerful exporting centres generating large trade surpluses. Keynes had wanted recip-rocal obligations on deficit and surplus countries but the Americans, then in surplus, had refused to agree. The result was that the powerful exporters could build up big surpluses, which damaged deficit countries like the UK (and, today, the US). Canny and cautious, the successful economies preferred to live below their means, building those large reserves rather than expanding their domestic economies. The US kept pressing the recalcitrants to revalue their currencies but with a total lack of success, and between 1996 and 2006, trade imbalances increased by five times.

This had two consequences for the less successful econo-mies, Britain and New Zealand. It heightened their problems as they binged on cheap imports, which had to be paid for by borrowing overseas, or by selling assets, companies and property to their successful competitors. It also made the successful countries eager to lend. Their surpluses couldn't just be piled up in massive reserves. They had to be invested somewhere and the obvious place was the irresponsibly importing countries – the US, Britain and New Zealand. So sovereign wealth funds and individual banks, companies and financiers loaned money to, and bought assets in the deficit countries, adding to the amount of money sloshing around in Britain, New Zealand and the US to keep them buying from the surplus-producing countries. In addition, reserve banks reduced interest rates to counter the intermittent crises. At each threat the US Federal Reserve Bank reduced interest rates. Money became cheap and plentiful.

The result was what Alan Greenspan, the head of the Fed, called "irrational exuberance", but is better described as a huge bubble blown up and sustained by ever-rising asset and house prices. As house prices rose people were pressured to take out bigger mortgages or to buy anything to get into the act and avoid paying rent. The banks were eager to indulge and help them regardless of the quality of the loan or the borrower. Mortgages took an ever-bigger share of bank lending and were sold on commission by salesmen who didn't care whether the purchaser was sub- or super-prime, because the salesman got commission and the mortgage could be bundled up and sold on as a CDO. These were bought by stupid investors, or what some American sellers described as "dumb German banks" (and British banks with the same low IQ but Savile Row tailoring), all eager to get in on the bonanza.

Here was a bubble based on ever-rising house and asset prices in defiance of the old economic law that bubbles will burst. Gordon Brown stuck to his claim that he had discovered a new paradigm of economic management which would banish boom and bust forever. In the American financial community, some at least knew the risk, but most didn't. Citibank, described by equities analyst and author Barry Ritholtz as "the biggest, stupidest and most irresponsible bank", kept on gambling because, as the chief executive of one bank put it, "While the music plays you gotta keep dancing."

In 2008, the music stopped. Purchasers of sub-prime mortgages who couldn't meet the payments began to walk out and return the keys to houses which then couldn't be sold, even at knock-down prices. The CDOs, whether rated AA or ZZ, ceased to produce a return. Desperate institutions sought credit to fund their rising debts but it had all dried up. Banks couldn't pay and the bubble burst. Bear Stearns in the US went first, then Lehman Brothers, one of the biggest CDO funders, went under, then AIG, who'd insured the bundles, and Freddie Mac and Fannie Mae, who'd guaranteed the mortgages. Panic radiated out from the US to Britain, France, Germany and all the other countries who'd joined the dance. Between 2007 and 2009, 20 banks in 10 countries had to be rescued. Credit dried up. The house of cards collapsed.

New Zealand was relatively immune. Its cautious,

Australian-owned banks hadn't gone to the ball but RBS, HBOS, Lloyds, Northern Rock and Bradford and Bingley in the UK all had full dance cards and had lent money beyond the limits of sense or reason. Too big to fail without disastrous consequences for the financial system as ATMs stopped issuing money, they had to be rescued by the government. In Iceland, all three banks had to be nationalised. So did the Irish banks.

The first reaction of politicians to a crisis is to panic. Britain's duly did. Mervyn King, the governor of the Bank of England, agonised about moral hazard and whether it was right to rescue people from their own follies, but the banks couldn't be allowed to go under. So the British government poured money out to save them. They were saved, but it led to a huge increase in the public debt. To stave off the collapse of the Icelandic banks and the withdrawal of their money, the British government in 2008 froze Icelandic assets under anti-terrorist legislation intended to stop money laundering. As a result of this folly, as chair of the Icelandic Parliamentary Group, I had to face (without any ministerial support) a mass protest of Icelandics parading across Westminster Bridge with signs saying "I'm a poet (or a bus driver or a construction worker) not a terrorist", and a refusal by Iceland to send the fish Grimsby depended on because our merchants couldn't pay for it. The banks wouldn't transfer the money. The President of Iceland later assured me that the hated figure of Gordon

Brown will be remembered in Iceland long after he's been forgotten in Britain.

The second reaction, however, was healthier. Governments dug Keynes out of the grave to which the monetarists had consigned him. Gordon Brown came good at last and persuaded the G20 that stimulus was the answer, then fluffed his announcement in the Commons by saying he'd saved the world (which was Blair's job). In 2008, President Obama, who'd just come into office and had a majority in Congress, persuaded it to pass a massive Recovery Act, spending on a New Deal scale, to start shovel-ready projects. Brown threw caution and his long love for prudence to the wind, boosted public investment, started to build the public housing for rent he'd long refused to countenance, and initiated a big building programme he'd previously argued could be financed only by PFIs.

It all started to work. Finance was steadied. In the first quarter of 2010, the new measures got growth back to an annualised rate of 3 percent. But it was too little, too late. In 2010, the G20 changed tack and opted for austerity. In Britain and New Zealand, recession, though milder in the latter than in Britain with its much bigger financial sector, undermined the appeal and credibility of the incumbent Labour parties. Electors tend not to like economic failure and higher unemployment. Brown in Britain had fumbled his chances by not calling an election in 2007 to renew his mandate. Helen Clark in New Zealand had faced a torrent of carping criticism that she had come to represent the Nanny State. Now both were thrown out. Though the conservative parties didn't actually win the elections in both countries they were able to form governments with coalition support. National and the Tories both came to power to resume the long march down Dead-End Street. The age of austerity began.

CHAPTER SEVEN

AUSTERITY

INITIALLY, MANY ON THE Left saw recession as an opportunity to get back to a Keynesian agenda and carry out reforms which would reverse the consequences of neoliberalism. As Rahm Emanuel, Democrat mayor of Chicago and President Barack Obama's first chief of staff, put it: "You never want a serious crisis to go to waste." He was dreaming of the restless search for new ideas and initiatives which had characterised President Franklin D. Roosevelt's New Deal in the US from 1932, just as British counterparts were thinking of the great burst of house building which had boosted their economy in the 1930s, and New Zealanders of the advent of the First Labour government in 1935.

All socialist pie in the sky. But also wrong. The first impact of the 1930s Great Depression had been to bring conservative governments to power almost everywhere, as frightened electorates turned not to the Left but to the Right and to the solutions conservatives offered. These were broadly summed up by poet A.R.D. Fairburn's description of Sir Otto

Niemeyer of the British Treasury, who visited New Zealand in the 1930s to advise the government what to cut and how to economise:

> The heart is gold, the name is Otto,
> 'Women and children first' the motto.

Now, this conservative reaction was even stronger than it had been in the 1930s. People were better off and felt they had more to lose. The bottom 59 percent of the New Zealand population had only 5 percent of the wealth but that meant that those above, two-fifths of the population, had 95 percent of it. They were scared. So they clung to orthodoxy not reform. One final factor explains the hegemony of the Right-wing incumbency. With the exception of the US, where recession occurred under George W. Bush's watch and had hit before Obama took over, elsewhere in the West – in Britain and most of Europe and in New Zealand – parties of the Left were in power. Most got thrown out.

Everywhere conservative parties won elections. The free-market liberals who had been chucked out when the electorate decided it was time for a rest, and had since searched in vain for new leaders, new policies and approaches, now came back to resume the process of liberalisation and complete their unfinished business. Thatcherism was back in power, with an even better excuse for its reforms.

Keynesian economics should come into its own in recession because stimulating demand by cheap money, public spending and investment in infrastructure and housing all offer boosts to a flagging economy of the type which had rescued the US with the New Deal, and Britain and New Zealand later in the 1930s. Keynesian expansion is well suited to an economy running below capacity. It had fallen into disrepute because, critics argued, Keynesian expansions to win elections when the economy became overstretched had led to inflation. This in turn produced the argument that interest rates should be taken out of the hands of the politicians and given to independent national banks, the managers of which of course knew what was virtuous and right. So Keynes had been locked up, away from the politicians.

The master's diagnosis was relegated to the junk room of history. Populist piggy-bank economics prevailed. People and governments viewed the national situation in personal terms, as if national debts and national borrowing were the same as personal debts on credit cards and personal borrowing through overdrafts. New Zealand had been built by borrowing spectacularly in the time of Premier Julius Vogel back in the 19th century, and continuously since. (An example was in 1928, when the ageing Prime Minister Joseph Ward misread his election speech. Ward had the ability to sway backwards and forwards when drunk, rather than side to side, but he had more difficulty in reading figures. He promised not a loan

103

of £7 million as his text prescribed but of £70 million, and promptly won the election.)

Personal debt is different. In both countries consumers and companies had maxed out on debt as demand was kept running at a higher level than productivity justified. The result was pain as people struggled to carry their personal burden. So the reaction of families and companies faced with debt is to batten down every available hatch, cut spending and embark on a regime of austerity. Inevitably they viewed national debts in the same way and conservative politicians were happy to reinforce this view.

In fact, public economics are different. There the individual's burden is the economy's boost. Because spending has a multiplier effect in boosting demand and puts people back to work, the best way to pay off debt is actually to borrow more, boost the economy and demand, and give money to the poor who spend it rather than to the rich who save. This brings down the weight of debt on the State because a bigger, richer economy can bear a heavier burden, a fact clearly illustrated by the way the huge war debts of Britain, much higher than today's post-recession debts, were paid off in the affluent 1950s because the economy expanded and inflation reduced the burden.

That was not allowed to happen under the neoliberal restoration. Debt was to be reduced as a central objective of policy because, for neoliberalism – as for Tea Parties, piggy-bankers and other assorted anti-state ideologues – it was the problem not the solution. Their answer was austerity: squeeze, freeze and cut to pay off the debt. Then an economy, freed from its burdens, would leap forward. Austerity was already the medicine prescribed for the Third World whenever their economies ran into difficulties. The International Monetary Fund (IMF) which then came in to help them prescribed a series of measures, collectively called the Washington Consensus.

This austerity prescription was in fact a massive dose of neoliberalism, of the kind which New Zealand and Britain had self-administered on a voluntary basis. Developing countries were told to end import and other controls, free capital inflows, welcome foreign investment, cut public spending and the taxes which raised it, sell off public enterprises and keep costs down by cutting wages. To get IMF help, failing economies had no alternative to taking this medicine, the only exception being Prime Minister Mahatir Mohamad in Malaysia, who stopped capital flows, imposed exchange controls and opted for a more mercantilist approach, which turned out to be more successful, despite the heavy censure he endured for refusing to take the IMF prescription.

Unfortunately for the patients, austerity had one major fault. Both common sense and economic theory indicated that a strong economy could endure austerity with only a small loss of growth, but that an already weak economy (as was the case in both Britain and New Zealand) would be further damaged. For such economies, the medicine couldn't and didn't work. Both nations endured it, just as patients in the Middle Ages had endured leeching, but the processes were painful and the patients didn't recover. Labour costs were cut on the grounds that lower wages would increase demand for workers, because labour was viewed as a cost, not a necessity or a benefit. The policy might have worked with potatoes, selling more as the price fell, but workers aren't potatoes. They are economic agents paying taxes when they're in work but needing support when they are not.

This had two consequences, which a fall in the price of potatoes doesn't. It cut demand, because the workers had less to spend, reducing the sales in shops and activity in the economy; it cut government revenues because the unemployed couldn't pay taxes. At the same time it increased government spending, because while potatoes could be dumped, workers couldn't be allowed to starve in the streets and had to be supported, thus increasing the deficit that austerity was meant to reduce.

Yet despite this inherent problem austerity became the norm in the advanced economies, in Britain and to a lesser extent in New Zealand, because governments saw it as the answer to the problems caused by recession. In Europe austerity was imposed for entirely different reasons, because it was forced on the poorer countries by the needs of the single currency which Europe had embarked on with joy and fireworks, the Euro.

This was an adventure the European Commission had begun under the presidency of Roy Jenkins in the 1970s, a time when the drive to unity was running down. To give the drive to ever-closer union a new dynamic, the Commission and Europe's leaders looked to a common currency. The first stage of that was an Exchange Rate Mechanism, which Britain declined to join initially, though it too came in much later. The idea was that this would be a discipline which gradually tightened as currency changes were ruled out, so that eventually Europe would find itself with one currency.

The Euro would then become the driver of union because a national currency for the whole of the membership would require new institutions, such as a European bank, a European budget and some kind of government machinery to coordinate national policies. It would, it was assumed, produce economic convergence between the members. Thus, it would achieve union by the back door without any necessity to seek consent from electorates or independent-minded governments still attached to their own powers. The plan didn't operate as smoothly as was hoped because in 1992 the ERM fell apart, sterling was driven out and the planners had to start again from scratch. This they did by the Maastricht Treaty, under which the Euro was launched in 2002. It provided that each new member of the EU would have to accept the single currency within five years of joining. In the event, Britain stayed out because Chancellor of the Exchequer Gordon Brown (who had supported joining the ERM), in his best contribution to history, saw the dangers of a single currency. In Denmark and Sweden referenda rejected membership.

The Euro was a project fine in theory, impossible in practice. The nation state is a natural base, some would say the only practicable base, for a currency union. A loose confederation of states at different levels of development is not. There are huge differences in productivity, inflation, competitiveness and economic power between Germany and the less developed areas like the "Club Med" states of Greece, Italy, Spain and Portugal. The Irish Republic, Mediterranean in its finances if not its weather, tagged along with them. Heavy investment, continuous improvement and *Mitbestimmung*, the co-determination between unions and business which keeps costs and wages down, meant that Germany combines enormous productive power and low inflation. The weaker states had neither. There, public spending was higher and productivity lower. There are only two ways in which nations in that situation could compete with Germany's superior power. They could cut costs and spending by a prolonged austerity, which might well have to go on for decades so great was the gap. Or they could devalue the currency to stimulate their exports and reduce their imports.

Up to that time periodic devaluations had been their

inevitable, and regular, choice. Ireland had devalued and broken away from its sterling tie, France had regular devaluations and even small ones in the ERM. The others had devalued even more regularly. Now they couldn't. Their exchange rate was inviolate, geared to German needs and fixed at the level Germany wanted. Never mind; this suited Germany. But not the lesser breeds without the *Wirfschaftwunder*, the economic miracle. Just as the Audi car company's assertion that "Vorsprung durch Technik" promised advancement through technology, in the European currency union, "austerity by Euro" was the only way for the laggards to stay competitive.

Nevertheless, the Euro was welcomed with a naive enthusiasm in 2002. Its first results were beneficial for all. The weaker nations got an economic boost. Money poured in because banks and investors assumed that a common currency the same as Germany's made investments outside Germany as safe as those inside. Unfortunately, it didn't. The others were not parts of a bigger, federal nation, but nation states in their own right with their own balances of payments, which were all adverse. They also had responsibility for their own debts, and these were huge and growing.

The result for all of them was a growing burden of debt, compounded in Greece by the fact that Greek ministers had fiddled their national accounts to get into the Euro in 2001. This was done with the willing collusion of the EU itself, so desperate its desire to get everyone in. As the initial euphoria evaporated, the uncompetitive Mediterranean states found themselves with a huge burden of debt, which in the case of Greece rose to well over 100 percent of GDP. There was no possibility of it ever being paid back because their economies weren't competitive or powerful enough to do so, but Germany and the EU both insisted that it had to be, and that the price of bailouts in 2010 and 2012 to tide it over was increasingly harsh doses of austerity.

Here was a problem common to all the Mediterranean states. Since they couldn't devalue, they now had to squeeze and freeze, cut government spending and company costs, and put people, particularly young people, out of work to depress demand and stop inflation rates always higher than Germany's. Europe had no central budget to redistribute spending towards them and no redistribution of the type nations use internally through regional policy, defence and infrastructure spending to boost regional growth. The costs would have fallen on Germany as the richest country but they would have been far, far bigger than that country, which had just managed at enormous cost to integrate East Germany with the West, was able to afford. German bankers had the simple view that debt is to be repaid, the German public was unsympathetic to scrounging Mediterraneans, so the most Euro-enthusiastic of nations wasn't prepared to pay and probably couldn't in any case.

Virtue is the German vice and in 2010 Chancellor Angela

Merkel set out to impose it on the weaker countries. The initial boom collapsed, leaving the Mediterraneans with the hangover. Spain had an unemployment rate of 25 percent. Young people there and everywhere faced mass unemployment. Mass emigration began from Greece, Portugal and Ireland – the latter losing 200,000 people. All this imposed intolerable strain on democratic electorates, who struggled to bear it and produced the rise of extremist parties of Right and Left in protest. It brought the Left to power in Greece in the form of the radical coalition Syriza, which vainly struggled against the regime imposed on it. In Portugal, the president initially refused to inaugurate the new government elected to stop austerity, then allowed it into office where, like Syriza, it found that it couldn't achieve its objective.

The resulting deflation even hit the powerful German economy, because its impoverished EU partners could no longer afford to buy the BMWs and Mercs they'd clamoured for in the initial prosperity. Far from eclipsing the dollar as an international currency and making the European economy stronger than America's, the Euro turned the Continent into the low-growth, high-unemployment black spot of the advanced world. This undermined Europe's ability to expand and grow to pull the world out of the Great Recession, and reduced its demand for the exports of other nations, particularly Britain, which supplied 50 percent of its exports to Europe.

Yet there was no way out. Germany insisted that the debts be paid back even if this was not possible. The debts couldn't be written off and protest parties like Syriza, when they came to power, weren't allowed to express the will of their people or ease the terms. Crowds demonstrated, workers struck, violence erupted and extremist parties grew, but Germany and the European Commission pressed on with their cruel regime. Europe had run right up against the Euro problem; it won't work and can't be made to. But it can't be allowed to fail. Europe is stuck. Unable to move forward or back.

The only attenuation allowed was when the despairing head of the European Bank announced that it would "do what it takes" to save the Euro. With Germany's grudging support, he began quantitative easing on a big scale. This helped European banks heavy with debt. It brought the Euro down in value to encourage exports. It led to asset inflation. But it couldn't provide the huge stimulus which was necessary to pull the EU out of its hole.

Thus, by a series of political accidents austerity became the norm, in greater or lesser degrees, in the West. In Europe, it resulted from the Euro. In Britain, it returned when the Conservative Party replaced Labour, which was attempting to rally the world to stimulus. The Tories didn't actually win the 2010 election but were better at not losing than Labour. They were confirmed in office when the Liberal Democrats agreed to a coalition. In the US, after an initial burst of stimulus, President Obama's hands were tied by a recalcitrant Republican Congress, which deadlocked politics and stopped further stimulus.

It was particularly severe in Greece, where it rose to intolerable levels after 2010, and in Britain where the new Conservative chancellor, George Osborne, portrayed his country as being in much the same mess. As a devotee of neoliberalism and Thatchernomics, Osborne seized the opportunity of power to resume the Thatcherite programme of rolling back the State, wiping out the debt and cutting government spending, to break inflation and the trade unions. He justified all this by arguing that Britain, like Greece, had maxed out its credit card to the point where it would soon be refused by world markets.

Austerity also hovered over Australia and New Zealand, though in a much-diluted form which was never as ideologically motivated nor as serious as the full-blooded neoliberalism of Roger and Ruth, because both countries were cushioned by their developing ties with China, the economy of which was growing at unprecedented rates. This produced bigger benefits for Australia, where the Lucky Country develops by digging up as much of itself as possible to sell, but both countries did better while the West suffered. Their banks, more tightly regulated and more profitable than their British and European counterparts, remained solid as mighty oaks fell elsewhere. So their economies grew while the rest flat-lined.

Austerity was the new norm, but the wrong answer. A

Keynesian answer to recession would have been to stimulate in order to spend. Some even advocated helicopter money, chucking it out of planes for the people to spend, a solution I would happily have endorsed had the helicopters hovered over Grimsby. Yet it was not to be. Borrowing was taboo, spending dangerous, cuts essential, democracy impossible, because the people couldn't be allowed to vote austerity out.

The banks were delighted to shift the blame for the crisis they'd created to the State which had saved them, or indeed onto anyone who became available. An electorate accustomed to thinking of public spending and debt in personal terms, as burdens to be reduced and paid off, accepted the logic of the State doing the same and knew nothing of Keynes's argument that public and private borrowing were not the same. Austerity was loudly preached by business and the better off and endorsed by most of the press. There was only one thing wrong. It wouldn't work and couldn't work.

At the simplest level, austerity freezes incomes, cuts benefits and forces people to borrow more to survive. All this slashes demand. People have less to spend. The basis of the post-war settlement had been to keep the economy growing by sustaining mass demand. That was now ended by a wholly unnecessary recession because the Conservative government used exactly the wrong weapons to deal with the situation. Instead of reflating it deflated, and instead of expanding it cut, which compounded the problem. Shops closed. In Britain, retail chains went bust – for instance, Woolworths in 2009 and Jessops in 2013. Sales fell, with a knock-on effect on production. Austerity, by increasing unemployment and freezing wages and household incomes, undermined the public finances because the tax take fell and government had to spend more to alleviate misery. So deficits grew, though the object of the exercise is to reduce them and stop public borrowing crowding out private. Low growth inevitably exacerbates inequality because the rich can better protect themselves. It makes competition for shares a zero-sum game. Austerity lowers expectations and hence investment. Boards and banks need better prospects ahead to encourage investment, but all they could see was endless gloom. Inevitably they battened down the hatches. Yet all these threats lay ahead as the world moved into the age of austerity, at the whim of the bankers.

CHAPTER EIGHT

THE REVENGE OF THE RICH

THROUGH 2008 AND 2009, Britain suffered five straight quarters of recession. British ministers who claimed that "We are all in this together" set out to swing the balances back to wealth. Austerity was both their weapon and their excuse. Like Rogernomics and Thatcherism, all this was done for ideological reasons, though these were stronger in Britain than in New Zealand.

In Britain, the dominant figure was not the prime minister, David Cameron, a genius at public relations who came to power in 2010. Cameron was adept at presenting misery as a preparation for unconfined joy and didn't believe in much, but would do anything to stay in power, where he believed his class belonged. Instead, the agent of austerity was his chancellor, George Osborne, the devout neoliberal who saw himself as a new Machiavelli with a mission to pay off the debt, close the deficit and get public expenditure down to 35 percent of GDP, rather than the 40 percent or more it had been under Labour.

New Zealand was better innoculated against neoliberalism. In 1996, it had adopted the Mixed Member Proportional representation system (MMP) for general elections, which requires broader consultation and makes it more difficult for the elective dictatorship to force more hard policies on the electorate. The neoliberal drive was now weaker because the prime minister, John Key, who took office in 2008, aimed at a kinder "good bloke" image – the nation's best mate – which was incompatible with being a Gradgrind or Scrooge, like Osborne. Key was a more traditional type of conservative, a wonderful actor able to speak with conviction all the parts the polls told him the public wanted. These included expressions of concern about the underclass and child poverty, though the warm words did not lead to any strong action.

Key's éminence grise was his minister of finance, Bill English – not as much of an ideologue as Osborne but a man who believed in the same, simple neoliberal verities of an independent central bank, "fiscal responsibility", and an under-run economy to control inflation and keep the workers in line. He was lucky in not facing the same problems of deficit and debt as Osborne had in Britain, because the previous Labour government had pursued a cautious financial policy, and English was really more of a Gladstonian than a neoliberal. So, he believed strongly in balanced budgets, eliminating deficits, repayment of debt, spending cuts to produce tax cuts and privatisation, but was under less pressure and had less justification for putting New Zealand back into the torture chamber.

His imperatives were much the same as Osborne's but were neither proclaimed with the same ideological zeal nor pursued with the same degree of fanaticism as in the UK. Nor were they as strong, because the Great Recession had hit New Zealand much less hard. In any case, ideology was less believeable because after the introduction of MMP, no New Zealand government could get away with an ideological crusade as Roger and Ruth had. Consequently, English accepted the need for a budget deficit to counter the recession and made only moderate changes to the tax regime by raising GST to 15 percent, cutting top tax rates and business taxes, and part-selling five state-owned enterprises. Benefits were maintained and the minimum wage slowly increased in the kind of budgets which might have been introduced by a National Party finance minister of the 1960s.

British austerity was both harsher and more cleverly sold. The new government created its own narrative to justify what it was doing. Vince Cable, a Liberal minister in the coalition government, claimed afterwards that Osborne was obsessed with shifting the blame for the crisis from the banks to the previous government and pinning the blame for excessive borrowing on Labour. He did so by claiming that the incoming government in 2010 faced a crushing burden of debt, at Greek levels, and that this came not as a result of saving the banks, but from Labour's irresponsible spending. Like Greece, the country was bust, a claim seized on from a jokey note left by an outgoing junior minister at the Treasury saying, "I'm afraid there is no money". Britain, Osborne claimed, was in imminent danger of having its credit card bounced on international markets.

None of this was true. Most of the debt was incurred by taking action to save the banks. Up to that point neither Labour's spending nor its borrowing had been unduly excessive. Both had been supported by David Cameron in 2008. But most of Osborne's claims were believed, a shaken Labour Party failed to tell its own side of the story, and the spin justified the resulting austerity. It was a classic propaganda exercise worthy of Lynton Crosby, who replaced Steve Hilton, the advocate of compassionate conservatism, as Cameron's chief adviser. Out went "Hug a hoodie", Cameron's call to show more understanding to disaffected hooded sweatshirt-wearing adolescents. In came the portrayal of the hoodie as an idle layabout needing to be taught, by benefit cuts, to get to work.

The propaganda also disguised the real motivation for the austerity programme on which Britain was now embarked. George Osborne as an ideological chancellor was comparable only with Ruth Richardson in the obsessive narrowness of his views, though he was far more effective in justifying them. He saw the purpose of government as being to roll back the State, cut public spending, and reduce taxes on the wealth generators, also known as the rich, his own class. He and his team of devoted acolytes controlled economic policy because his friend Cameron was a nonchalant leader who preferred "chillaxing" and holidays to obsessive interference. Cameron left his ministers to get on with their jobs. He should have understood economics better, having taken a degree in PPE (philosophy, politics and economics) at Oxford, while his chancellor was a mere ten-a-penny history graduate. But he delegated the whole field to his first mate and best friend. The cuts began immediately.

Benefits were reduced to do the disabled and unemployed the favour of being jolted out of the dependency culture to which Labour had reduced them. Investment plans were slashed, cutting back infrastructure plans, including the road programme and a flood-defence scheme, which had been enlarged to combat the threat from global warming. The council-house building programme which Gordon Brown had started was stopped. Local government was put on such thin gruel that even Tory councils began to protest, though the cuts were slanted so that they got off more lightly than Labour authorities. Public servants were put on a pay freeze and government departments instructed to slash their budgets. Only the education, health and overseas aid budgets escaped, protected by the election manifesto, though the National Health Service was burdened with the cost of a massive reorganisation (which the Tory manifesto had promised not

to do). This was done to save money, though it cost more than
£1 billion to reshuffle everything again in order to open it up
for private providers, who then didn't come. The tertiary sector
wasn't included in education, so the government was able to
shift more of the costs of the universities onto the shoulders of
students by allowing the institutions to raise fees from £3000
a year, the figure at which Labour had capped them, to £9000.
Most universities duly put them up to the maximum.

The result was a shock to the system, a drastic cut of
400,000 in the number of public servants and the decline in
economic growth from an annual rate of 3 percent in the first
quarter of 2010 to zero by the end of the year. All this produced
a fall in the projected deficit soon reversed by another in
government's income, because the newly jobless ceased to pay
taxes and went on benefits, which increased spending. Public
services were farmed out to new private organisations which
claimed to be able to run them more cheaply, cost the government less and still make a profit. Unfortunately, though, their
performance was not as distinguished as their propaganda.
ATOS, the French company brought in to assess whether
sick and disabled beneficiaries were able to go back to work,
certified 2380 people as capable of work between 2011 and
2014, only to see them die within a month of having their
allowance cut, causing critics to claim that their 10-question
assessment form should be reduced to a simple one of, "Are
you dead?"

Branches of A4E, the body responsible for getting people back to work, whose founder made £8 million out of it and became a government adviser, claimed bonuses for people it had merely parked in self-employment. G4S, brought in to provide security at the Olympic Games, messed up completely and had to be replaced by troops. Serco, which took over tagging prisoners, claimed for thousands it hadn't actually tagged. Local government closed libraries, swimming pools, sports facilities, youth services and 700 children's centres and cut down on rubbish collections (which was good for rats and rates but not litter). Police numbers fell. Even the armed services were cut back at a time when they were over-extended in Iraq and Afghanistan. Not exactly a distinguished record, but one which saved money, at the cost of reducing the quality of life, undermining public services and producing grief for beneficiaries.

The impact of this was reduced by another piece of propaganda. Where pre-war unemployment had produced a welling up of public sympathy, the victims of austerity got less because they were portrayed as the victims of their own idleness, and as scroungers (bludgers in New Zealand) leeching off the taxes of the hard-working community. Now the loss of jobs and benefit was supposed to help them by forcing them out of dependence for their own good so they could stand on their own feet in jobs which didn't exist. Once again this was spin, but widely believed by a nation palsied by fear, its charitable instincts dulled by the spirit of every man for himself.

The description "hard-working families" became obsessively used. It was always set in contrast with the idleness of "scroungers". Several ministers described moving scenes of the hard workers going out to their hard work on cold winter mornings angered by seeing scrounging neighbours still abed, and presumably procreating to bring more children into the world and increase the family's benefit income, which was all paid for by the over-burdened hard workers.

The economies were massive and more than enough to pay for the reduction in the top rate of tax which accompanied them. But the promise of growth and a balanced budget achieved through the pain was not fulfilled. It couldn't be, because the spending and benefit cuts reduced demand; shops went bankrupt. Manufacturing continued to decline, as did the government's tax take. Osborne's promise to eliminate the debt by 2015 became unattainable. It had to be put back to 2020, not too difficult a deferment because few had believed it anyway. In fact, elimination was impossibly difficult because the price of deindustrialisation had to be paid. The death of manufacturing in the old industrial heartlands of Scotland and the North and Midlands meant that their once productive workforces now had to be supported by benefit spending, wages top-ups, tax credits and unemployment benefits. Two economists from Sheffield Hallam University calculated that this new reverse Danegeld ran at between £20 billion and £30 billion a year, or almost half of the fiscal deficit. This had to be paid to the old heartlands just to keep them going at a lower and more miserable level than industry had formerly maintained.

The result of not eliminating the debt was three years of almost zero growth and rising unemployment, a disastrous downturn from which the government was rescued not by its own efforts (which are always to persevere with punishments) but by the Bank of England. Having reduced the bank rate to half of 1 percent at the onset of recession it kept it there for the longest period in British history. Such a reduction was bound to produce some recovery along with the rising house prices it also led to. Yet the economy was in so bad a state that the Bank of England now took a further step by doing what it had always claimed would be disastrous and as ruinously inflationary as the Weimar Republic's inflation. It began to print money and created, in all, £375 billion of new cash by quantitative easing, a process of buying back public debt from the banks which held it, which gave them massive sums of cash to put in their reserves and, hopefully, to lend to business to invest. The greedy banks kept most of it for themselves, which at least safeguarded their weak position, but some of it did get into stimulus spending and helped hold down an exchange rate, which was rising, and boost confidence, which was scarce. However, much of that confidence had the effect of boosting house and asset prices, compounding the growing housing problem.

Economic policy was being run at cross-purposes, with an expansionary bank compensating by its lax monetary policy for a recessionary chancellor's fiscal overkill. Inevitably the bank's stimulus and the passage of time did produce recovery, starting in 2013. It was weaker and slower than recovery from previous recessions. It came mainly from ever-rising house prices and increased consumer spending financed by debt, rather than the "march of the makers" which Osborne had promised. More than half the new jobs created went to Eastern Europeans lured to Britain by the fact that, weak as it was, the British economy was at least doing better than the Continent caught in the Euro trap. By 2015 growth was back to the 3 percent annual rate which Gordon Brown had managed to achieve in the dying days of the Labour government. That was just in time for the government to claim it as the result of what they now called their "long-term economic plan" and hold an election. The Conservative government got an unexpected majority of 12, enough to junk its coalition partners, the Liberals, who had lost 50 seats as the price of loyally supporting economic folly for five years. Now the Conservatives were in a position to govern alone, ready to lead the country into the next round of austerity.

In New Zealand, more than 60 finance houses failed between 2006 and 2012, robbing savers of some $9 billion, but overall the country was in a much less difficult economic situation. The economy wasn't in as bad a state as Britain's thanks to the opening up of the rapidly growing Chinese market. The Labour government hadn't had to pour millions into the banks to save them because they'd been cautiously run while government itself had been financially cautious, and had maintained fiscal balance with growth still running at around 3 percent. There was no possibility of blaming a policy of slash and burn on a mess left by the outgoing government.

John Key's National government was far less ideological. A rich man risen from a poor background, Key knew the world of the underclass in a way no British prime minister ever could and in his eagerness for power he had in any case tied his government's hands by promising to retain most of the changes made by Labour and to stop privatisation. Much of the business community still looked to neoliberalism but the flame burned much lower than in the 1990s.

Key was also more cunning than his predecessors. His motivations were better concealed. He gave business interests his top priority and social issues second rank. He aimed to privatise more assets and cut public spending to give tax cuts to the rich. Yet he did it all more gradually, believing (and finding) that neoliberalism could be acceptable if it was advanced in small stages rather than by Roger Douglas's quantum leaps. Policies were floated, public opinion was sounded and changes were implemented only if they proved acceptable. This wrong-footed a Labour opposition with a bad conscience, which made it unable to resist his policies without calling their own record into question. In contrast with the messianic approach of previous governments this backdoor neoliberalism proved both more acceptable and less damaging.

In any case, New Zealand had a much easier ride than Britain, with growth and lower unemployment. The MMP system would have made it difficult if not impossible to go for austerity but New Zealand didn't need it. As a result, discipline in New Zealand was milder and had less painful consequences than in the UK. The country was successfully widening its trading relationships but a slowing Chinese economy forced achieving a permanent budget balance to be put back to 2020. Indeed, the National Party's first budget in 2009 was almost Keynesian, with a $5.8 billion boost to stimulus spending, a tax cut and the promise of further tax reductions ahead.

In each country Labour oppositions wavered uncertainly, unable to decide whether to protest against austerity, oppose the more substantial cuts, or try to make themselves respectable by deference to business, to tax cuts and to lower public spending. In this uncertain situation both Labour parties were hit by election defeats. In Britain, where austerity had been harshest, Labour expected to be carried to power in

2015 by a wave of protest against cuts and low growth. In fact, it lost Scotland, which rejected both English parties and elected Nationalists for nearly every seat. Labour failed to make ground elsewhere and the Conservative government was strengthened by winning seats from its Liberal Democrat partners. The Conservatives' 12-strong majority was enough to govern alone in an electoral system which allows governments to skate on very thin ice and carry on skating even after the ice melts. Once installed the government took immediate steps to strengthen its position by reducing the Commons by 50 seats through a redistribution which favoured the Tories, purging the electoral registers and cutting off Labour funding from both the unions and the State.

In New Zealand, the National Party did even better. In the 2014 election it achieved the difficult task under MMP of getting a majority, enough to govern on its own, though it did take the added precaution of enrolling the support of the inevitable and invincible Peter Dunne.

The two economies were diverging. As New Zealand gave up on austerity Britain plunged in deeper with a new dose. George Osborne slashed the tax credits subsidising low wages and the housing benefits protecting tenants. He began to force housing associations to sell off their properties as the councils had done before, and set out to impose income limits on people in public sector rented properties to turn them into ghetto housing for the poor. He cut benefits and required every department except education and health to cut spending by almost a third and local government to cut by 24 percent over five years. Both tasks were painful and nearly impossible, particularly if they were to expand social services to alleviate the pressures on the health service.

A daunting five years loomed ahead. The British Labour Party reacted to defeat in 2015 in the way it had done after previous defeats in 1951 and 1979, by embarking on an internal civil war. This resulted in the election, by a rank and file well to the Left of the parliamentary party, of Jeremy Corbyn, the man of a thousand causes who now had to narrow his visions to one: getting Labour elected, which became more difficult under his leadership. The Right of the party began a prolonged sulk while the media set out to destroy Corbyn. Many on the Right refused to join his shadow cabinet. Several who were appointed deserted and, before the 2016 summer recess, an overwhelming majority of the Parliamentary Labour Party voted no confidence in its leader, precipitating another leadership election. Labour was pioneering felo de se, or suicide, as a political strategy, and the problem was compounded when Corbyn was re-elected with an increased majority after a futile challenge. The huge new membership received this rapturously but their approbation couldn't transform Corbyn into an election-winning leader.

This collapse of the official opposition made it easy for the government to pass anything it wanted. The trade unions were too weak to do anything much about it and government took no notice of the spluttering protests in the community. Only the House of Lords, where the Conservatives didn't have the same majority as they did in the Commons, had the power to resist and it did indeed nerve itself up to reject cuts in tax credits for workers. Osborne denounced the coup as unconstitutional and promptly made up the money lost by cuts in housing benefits.

In New Zealand, as its terms of trade grew worse and China slowed, the National government embarked on another dose of medicine. In 2009–2010 it increased GST to 15 percent, but cut income tax and through 2013 to 2014 began a partial sale of assets, ignoring a referendum which showed most people were opposed to them. John Key was able to ignore the 2013 referendum because of the low turnout. The government also flirted with the idea of targeted benefits rather than general improvements and turned to a round of regulatory reforms to make the country even more fit to do business. The only economic saving grace in these years was an act of God. A series of earthquakes did enormous damage to Christchurch; 185 people were killed when a large quake occurred on 22 February 2011. The huge task of reconstruction, though slow and excessively bureaucratic because government took control of the rebuild from the local community, required enormous public spending; about $16 billion of the $40 billion cost of reconstruction was to come from the government's coffers.

Keynes had once argued that government could stimulate the economy by paying people to dig holes. Now Christchurch became the new Keynesian boost for New Zealand. Government was forced into a massive stimulus programme to repair and rebuild the new Christchurch. This new stimulus programme prompts the suggestion that the fallen statue of John Robert Godley, founder of the city, in Cathedral Square should be replaced by one of John Maynard Keynes, triumphant over austerity. The repaired statue of Godley was re-erected, however, even though nearly six years after the earthquake the Christchurch central business district still looked less than half finished.

CHAPTER NINE

REPORT ON EXPERIENCE

OVER THE SIX-YEAR period between 2007 and 2013, the British economy failed to grow even at the modest rates it had reached in the past. Growth was either lost to the Great Recession or needlessly thrown away by the austerity programme. The failure to reflate, the new dose of neoliberal cuts and the deliberate under-running of the economy all diluted human resources. Employment became more casual in the "gig economy" of reduced worker rights. In 2005, before George Osborne's great reform-by-punishment programme got under way, unemployment had been under 4.5 percent. Within seven years, it was hitting 8 percent. Such figures would have been regarded with horror in the post-World War II years; now they were treated as normal, even inevitable, almost a desirable discipline for the government but a punishable offence for the workers, as if the unemployed were choosing idleness as a lifestyle.

This waste of people undermined the public finances. With higher unemployment, less tax is paid and more has to be paid out in support and benefits, a problem compounded by the loss of high-paid jobs in manufacturing and the growth of low-paid casual and part-time employment, not to mention the growing number encouraged to become self-employed and go slowly bankrupt, to get them off benefit. A policy aimed at reducing debt increases it because of the costs of misery.

This makes the goal of a balanced budget a mirage constantly vanishing ahead of us, though that's merely a recognition of reality, because balancing the budget is the last thing a government should do when the economy is in recession. Better to run a deficit and spend to stimulate. It's daft to tie yourself to balancing it, as Bill English did in New Zealand and George Osborne did in the UK. Who can tell what the state of the economy will be then and whether or not the government needs to borrow to stimulate growth?

The problem which aroused more complaint and most interest was the increase of inequality as a result of low growth, the Friedmanite triumph and the processes of managing the economy through meddling in the money supply. Markets favour the strong anyway, because they have more power and resources than the mass of the people. So the rich became much richer, the poor poorer relatively, and the living standards of the mass of the people were kept down as their incomes flat-lined.

The resulting divergence is clear in both the US and

Britain, the two countries where it is worst. In both, attention has concentrated on the increase in the wealth and power of the top 1 percent, a process best described in the Oxford social geographer Danny Dorling's book *Inequality and the 1%*, which shows that the share of national income taken in Britain by the top hundredth of the population has increased from 5 percent when Margaret Thatcher came to power to 15 percent. In New Zealand, it rose from 5 percent to 9 percent. The 1 percent have far more wealth than the bottom 50 percent. The pay of the chief executives of the top 100 companies shot up and by 2015 averaged £5.5 million. By 2016, counting pensions and bonuses, their average pay was 129 times that of the average worker. Martin Sorrell, chief executive of an advertising agency, took home £67 million, the CEO of BP, £14 million. Both ignored share holder votes against such obscene sums. Meanwhile, the Gini coefficient, the internationally agreed measure of income equalities, shows the greatest widening in Britain (and specifically in London, home of at least 80 billionaires) and the US; the least, incidentally, was in Iceland and Norway. In New Zealand, it remained fairly stable after widening in the years of Rogernomics.

The question which arises is, can we afford the rich? They unbalance society. They are both privileged and unaccountable. They answer only to themselves. In Iceland and Ireland bankers went to jail for their part in the 2008 collapse. In Britain, the only sanction was that two people lost knighthoods they hadn't deserved in the first place. The Establishment protected its own and took everyone back into highly paid jobs. The rich can employ high-powered accountants to manage their affairs so that they pay proportionately less in tax than most workers. Multi-billionaire Warren Buffett pointed out that he paid tax in the US at a lower rate than his receptionist. So do many millionaires in Britain, where receptionists are paid less than in America.

As for the banks, the people who caused the crash and who were caught out in various scams, like the manipulation of interest rates and the mis-selling of pensions, were still paying themselves huge bonuses and dodging their tax liabilities. Efforts to tighten up regulation were largely abandoned. In 2015, the seven largest investment banks paid only £21 million in tax on the £3.6 billion profits they made in Britain.

In Britain, the financial classes largely regulate themselves in accountancy, banking, the City and the law. They buy places in the House of Lords. They influence policy by contributing to political parties, particularly the Tories, and influence public opinion because they own most of the newspapers, while the power of the workers has been sadly diminished. The unions have been broken.

Gaps widen for two reasons. The top goes up. The bottom either falls or remains stationary. That's exactly what has been happening. The first part of the equation is explained by two economic laws. The first is set out by French rock-star economist Thomas Piketty, whose book *Capital in the Twenty-First Century* stands Marxism on its head. Marx predicted the diminishing of profits, which would eventually produce such pressure on the working class that it would lead to revolution. On the contrary, Piketty argues that wealth grows faster, because of compounding interest, than economic growth, which of course has been lower than it used to be. In Britain and the US, the share of income taken by the top 1 percent has doubled since 1980. It hasn't in other countries.

Piketty could have added that profits have risen because of the obsession with shareholder value, which involves squeezing the maximum profit out of companies because that determines the rewards to the top executives in share bonuses and profit-related pay. CEO pay has risen faster and further in the US and UK than in any other country and more than 80 CEOs in Britain are paid more than £1 million a year, while many others get golden parachutes if they fail. In 2015, British companies paid out £44.3 million in bonuses to top employees while the pay of the workers remained relatively flat.

Secondly, we can add to this the theory advanced by Robert Reich, the American economist who was President Bill Clinton's labour secretary. In his book *Saving Capitalism* he calls the now-dominant big corporations not just monopolistic, but monosponic – they are the only buyers in the market. They have purchasing power over labour and political power through their control of the media, and through buying the politicians who depend on their contributions. They've been able to use legislative power to shackle the unions, reduce their own taxes and corporation tax and to shuck off social and environmental obligations. They've been weakening the State, shackling its efforts and changing the whole system to suit their selfish interests.

At the same time as those at the top have been set free to enrich themselves, those at the bottom have been shackled. Cuts in benefits and welfare have reduced their incomes, the trade unions which advanced their cause have been weakened so far as to be largely irrelevant in New Zealand, while they've been broken and tied down by law in Britain. Economic developments have also hit incomes, for the decline of manufacturing, particularly in Britain and New Zealand, has eliminated a lot of work and highly-paid jobs, and the countervailing development of service jobs such as tourism in New Zealand hasn't replaced them. Service jobs, whether in supermarkets, restaurants or hotels, tend to be lower paid than digging coal or making steel.

Immigration became a major issue as two million new workers came in to the UK, mainly from Eastern Europe. The government promised to get net immigration down to 100,000 a year. In fact, it exceeded 330,000 in 2015. David

Cameron argued that the immigrants were lured from Eastern Europe by benefits. Instead, they came for jobs which aren't available in Euro-crushed Europe. Immigration on this scale has the effect of holding down wages. So does offshoring to lower-cost countries, while mechanisation and computerisation have eliminated both heavy labour and repetitive work. All this combines to mean that the steady improvement in household incomes which characterised the 1950s and 1960s has ground to a halt, while the incomes of what Americans call the great middle class (and the more snobbish Britons call the working and lower-middle classes) have been largely stationary for several decades. Only redistribution and government action could have remedied this and that's been largely lacking. It's no wonder therefore that all the social balances have been shifted in favour of wealth while economic gaps have been widened. Appropriately the share of Gross Domestic Product going to salaries and wages fell by up to 15 percent in the UK, rather less in New Zealand, while the share going to profits and dividends rose over the last 20 years.

Another result has been the increase in comparative poverty despite the efforts of Labour governments to cushion the income of the low-paid by tax credits. More people were kept afloat by growing debt on credit cards and through expensive pay-day lenders. There was a huge increase in the number of op-shops, or charity shops. Meanwhile, charities and local initiatives began providing breakfasts and lunches to children at school. In the weeks before Christmas 2015, the Auckland City Mission was handing out 3000 food parcels, a third of them to new claimants, which is something I never expected to see in New Zealand.

Paradoxically the banks were awash with money but boosting the share of their lending going to mortgages at a time when fewer houses and very little state housing for rent were being built. Neoliberal governments disinvested in housing, particularly in public housing for rent, the mainstay of the less well off. In Britain, every government up to 1979 had built large numbers of council houses. The Conservative-led government after 2010 built fewer every year. Building more would have meant borrowing, even though it created an asset for local authorities, and the Tories regarded council estates as breeding grounds for Labour voters. The inevitable result was rapid growth in the price of private houses. So the proportion of both nations owning their own houses fell by up to 10 percent as house prices rose beyond the reach of two-fifths of the population. Lots of big expensive houses were being built (particularly in London, where there's an insatiable demand from funny money manipulators, investment funds, sheiks and oligarchs), but few affordable ones and practically no public rental housing. Later on, as an unprecedented housing problem developed, the Cameron government tried to tackle it by "help to buy" schemes. Since fewer private houses were being built than in the affluent years this fueled the price rise.

The average house price in London in 2014 was £443,399, compared to £150,851 in the North. The general increase has been running at 7 percent, though the old economic law that if something can't go on forever it probably won't must come into effect at some stage. *The Guardian* has calculated that for anyone earning the national average wage of £26,500, 91 percent of houses in England and Wales are unaffordable. High prices in London are leading to a kind of socio-economic cleansing as the workers have had to move out of the city, away from their jobs.

The same process is going on at lower levels in Auckland, where 40 percent of new houses are bought by foreigners and the median house price is now $1 million, so the poor are driven out ever further to poorer suburbs, traffic and travel to work increase and the rich dominate the central city. The median house price in Dunedin was $348,000 in 2016. Marvellous to move south if you can bring your own weather, but a wider gap than that between house prices in London and, say, Yorkshire, where people can live more cheaply but find it more difficult to get work.

In August 2016, the International Monetary Fund said that New Zealand had the highest house price to income ratio in the developed world. Prices have been increasing at a rate of 10 percent a year, particularly in Auckland, which creates a disastrous situation for the growing proportion who can't pay such prices, can't get mortgages and for whom very little is being built in the way of public housing for rent, or state or council houses. The percentage of home owners has declined in both Britain and New Zealand, and many more people are condemned to live as "generation rent" in a largely unregulated and insecure rental market. In Britain, 5.4 million households live in the private rental sector. In New Zealand, the poorest fifth of families pay 40 percent of their income in rent, while in Britain's major cities the numbers of rough sleepers outdoors were estimated to have doubled in 2016. So much for a home-owning democracy.

Poverty on the scale we now see in both countries means more people excluded from the national life and more deprived children. New Zealand is a great place to bring up children (before they go off to Australia), but the Children's Commissioner reports that a third of New Zealand children live below the poverty line. Jonathan Boston, of Victoria University of Wellington, who's both the best expert and the agony aunt of child poverty, estimates that it's between 120,000 and 260,000 (depending on whether you count 50 or 60 percent of national income as poor). So let's say there are, conservatively, 200,000 out of 1 million kids living in poverty. That means they're partially excluded from the Kiwi world by bad health, bad housing and bad diet, all compounded by the inadequacies of under-resourced schools and services in both ghetto estates and rural slums.

In New Zealand, child poverty is double the level of the 1980s and higher than in most countries, including Great Britain. It's also appalling. You can argue that most poverty is relative rather than absolute. If you're particularly mean-minded you can argue, as John Key has, that poverty arises because parents are too whacked out on drugs to work. Maybe some are. But most aren't, and all children in poverty, whether Mum's a smack-head or a battered angel, are at risk and will become a cost to society as they grow up.

The effect of poverty is not only that it's socially bad, but that it's economically inefficient. It fails to develop all talents. It reduces demand. More money going to the rich means more spending on imports like BMWs, more on ostentatious houses and more to pass on to their spoiled brats. More money going to the poor is spent on basic necessities, locally produced, or even at Mitre 10 for DIY home improvements, all of which boosts demand and stimulates production.

These problems are compounded when poverty hits some ethnic groups harder than others, as it demonstrably does in Britain. There, black people and Pakistanis suffer far more from it than whites and in New Zealand poverty and unemployment are much higher among Maori and Pasifika than among Pakeha. The Maori unemployment rate was 12 percent in 2012, double the Pakeha rate, and the Pasifika rate was higher still. These are developments disastrous for any good society but positive discrimination to reverse them arouses outcry from the white majority, like the protests about busing to transport children from racial minorities to better schools in Britain and the US, or the hysteria over the Waitangi settlement and the foreshore and seabed argument in New Zealand. Discrimination in favour of disadvantaged groups is politically difficult.

When Maori were a largely rural population no one particularly bothered about the poverty they lived in. Then the Hunn Report of 1961 and Ans Westra's *Washday at the Pa*, a photographic school publication in 1964, served to bring home the disadvantages faced by rural Maori. Since then the Maori drift to the towns and its consequences, as described in Alan Duff's novel *Once Were Warriors* (exaggerated perhaps, but still shocking), have brought the problem home. The Waitangi settlement process paid a debt of honour, though hardly in full, by endowing a traditional Maori elite with resources and enterprises. However, it did little for the impoverished urban Maori living outside traditional structures. It doesn't help the Pasifika population at all.

Learning Maori, boosting their culture and calling the country Aotearoa-New Zealand are all empty gestures if a large section of Maori and Pasifika are relegated to an underclass in poorer suburbs with higher unemployment, worse conditions and worse prospects than those of the Pakeha.

New Zealand's over-large prison population (double the proportion of most civilised countries – a category which doesn't include Britain) has a proportion of Maori which exceeds the proportion of black people in prison in America. Here's a problem which can only be dealt with by special measures and dedicated support to close the gaps and boost Maori and Pasifika education. However much the Pakeha may grumble. This isn't to say that nothing should be done for the white majority underclass too. They need pulling up as well. No nation can afford to waste and deprive so many people, or see the growth of the kind of lumpen deprived working-class left in Britain's industrial areas and the former one-industry towns where the industry has been destroyed.

Another major consequence of our 40 wasted years of wrong-headed economics has been the decline of manufacturing, which provides the major share of exports in Britain and has maintained import substitution in New Zealand. In Britain, manufacturing declined in number of jobs, in power and in the contribution it made to the balance of payments. British manufacturing was deeply damaged by EU membership and New Zealand's rather less so by Closer Economic Relations (CER) with Australia, while in Britain this was compounded by an exchange rate kept too high for far too long. Once 30 percent of the economy in Britain at the start of the period, manufacturing had declined to 10 percent by the end. The first workshop of the world became the fastest to de-industrialise, creating huge costs in benefits and support for the old industrial heartlands. In New Zealand, CER began reductions in tariffs, which were almost all gone by the end of the 20th century. Much domestic production simply went out of business or transferred to Australia once tariff and import controls were eliminated and manufacturing's share of GDP fell even more than in Britain.

The result in both countries, but particularly Britain, has been to undermine the economic base of society. Areas of Britain where industry was based, particularly the North, have been desolated: they remain sadly run down, depressed areas of high unemployment. The young are forced to seek work in London or further afield. In New Zealand job opportunities have likewise been restricted, increasing the allure of greener pastures in Australia. As a consequence, the North of England has been left to oldies like me and New Zealand has lost its image as a young country. Instead, it has become a land where the old stay on for National Super and the young, who're effectively being asked to pay for it, leave. No wonder. In both countries, the young got much the worse deal out of neoliberalism. None of the benefits enjoyed by the Baby Boomer generation came to them.

The inevitable result of this decline has been gaping balance-of-payments deficits. New Zealand had always run one to finance development, but Britain paid its way in the world until the 1980s, when the gap opened, and has steadily widened since. Imports grew, and exports lost competitiveness and declined. The performance of British goods and cars in the New Zealand market is the classic illustration. So-called manchester goods (household linen) now come from the Phillipines. British cars which once dominated the New Zealand roads have lost out to the Japanese and Europeans. By 2015 Britain was running a deficit of 6 percent of GDP; New Zealand 2 percent.

Unprecedented deficits on this scale can only be financed by overseas borrowing, which grew rapidly, turning the flow of investment income which rentier Britain had relied on into a negative drain, souring the balance of payments and drawing demand from the economy. The other way of financing deficits is by the sale of assets, firms, farms, property citizenship and privatised utilities, or by attracting wealth, however iffy its source. London is effectively for sale and much of the new building is going towards luxury properties costing between £2 million and £40 million, which only dodgy money merchants, or Tony Blair, could afford.

In both countries foreign ownership has increased, is increasing and ought to be diminished. The proportion of foreign ownership in New Zealand is among the highest of countries in the advanced world. Foreigners bought up some of the British assets privatised by Margaret Thatcher, such as water and airports, but they bought much more in New Zealand, where few domestic buyers could raise the money for assets on that scale. All but six of New Zealand's 24 registered banks are foreign-owned. Australians, whose banks are the world's most profitable, control the New Zealand banking system and the issue of credit, and only one main-centre daily newspaper, the *Otago Daily Times*, is now New Zealand owned.

In Britain, all the major car manufacturers and several of the privatised utilities, such as Thames Water, owned by Macquarie Bank, are foreign-owned. In each country, this means the export of profits, research, design and power, which in turn reduces both demand and the market for skills and careers in the host country. Free marketeers argued that ownership is irrelevant. It isn't. Profits are extorted then exported, reducing demand at home and making an always-precarious balance of payments worse. Foreign companies have less interest in local markets and local needs. When the parent company faces difficulties, its foreign subsidiaries are the first to be shut down. Their labour force is easier to shed, particularly in New Zealand and the UK, where job protection and redundancy provisions are much weaker than in most countries.

With more foreign ownership the last and loneliest part of a multinational can become the most exploited, priced out and badly served. New Zealand has already found this out in banking and telecommunications, which have been highly profitable milch cows for overseas owners. Where Roger Douglas hoped that privatised Telecom (since renamed as the aspirational but less-than-bright Spark) would earn millions in exports, its achievement has been limited to taking millions out of the country in profits. Performance in broadband, which New Zealand needs more than most to plug into the wider world, has been slow compared to other countries, even allowing for the tyranny of distance. People who think they've got wi-fi haven't really. Digital optical fibre installation has been slow. Broadband is over-charged when too much of it is charged by megabyte units per month. That reduces use and ensures that the more you use the more you pay, with the addition of a cap which increases the charge. The private sector has been slow in the introduction of broadband, which has had to have State funding to boost the pace of installation and the coverage of this vital means of connecting New Zealand with everywhere else. In the summer of 2016 I drove into Lawrence in Otago, past signs boasting "New Zealand's first wired up town". When I attempted to use my computer, nothing happened. The tea room proprietor explained this, saying, "Someone else must be using it." It made the broadband revolution seem more like the old days of "party line" shared telephone connections.

As manufacturing and domestic industry declined, Finance, the great gambling force which grows by risk not production, has boomed. Always strong in Britain, it has become so dominant that some argue that services and Finance are the national future, capable of closing the growing deficit. Finance may be more glamorous, exciting and far better paid than metal bashing or other honest work, but the number of jobs it offers is small and totally out of proportion to the loss of manufacturing jobs. Finance poses a far greater threat of instability. As long as manufacturing paid the nation's way, Britain's upper class could become idle rentiers. Once manufacturing failed their world had no foundation. Capital is free to move, and with electronic transfers it moves instantly. Production and people are less flexible, with the result that an economy with a weakening manufacturing sector and a growing and speculative financial sector is increasingly vulnerable. In Britain, the return on Britain's investments overseas has turned negative, making Britain a debtor nation on a growing scale.

Money flowing in from elsewhere is greeted by ministers as confidence in the country. And in them. Yet it can flow out just as easily and quickly and a currency with no visible means of support, which others have in their powerful exporting bases, is exposed to short selling and a collapse of confidence, both of which can come suddenly. That could require interest rates to rise, inflicting great damage on a country kept afloat by debt. Such an outflow is now a real danger for both economies but particularly Britain's. In 1992, George Soros made billions out of the collapse of the pound when Britain was forced out of the ERM, just as, on a smaller scale, others in Citibank made millions out of selling the Kiwi dollar short.

This growing dependence on financial inflows undermined the tax system in the UK. The British government turns a half-blind eye to tax evasion and avoidance by rich incomers and multinationals, who smuggle profits out to low tax jurisdictions to avoid paying the social rent they owe in Britain. So the money flows into and out of London and around the world are immense, and the dangers which produced the Great Recession are still there, implicit in that free flow of money which is easy-come, easy-go. Ministers argue that there's no problem. Confidence will be sustained as long as they run the economy on neoliberal lines. On the contrary, the market facilitates speculation and to defend the currency is to reward the speculators. Any nation that can't pay its way faces the prospect of currency falls, as at some stage it must if trade is to be balanced. Indeed, that fall in the exchange rate has already begun in Britain as a consequence of the shock of the Brexit vote. With such a fall the whole delicate recovery could be endangered, consumers and companies weighed down by debt might be crucified and confidence could collapse. Only a recovery solidly based on the revival of manufacturing and the rebalancing of the economy from its excessive dependence on Finance – by the growth of the production and construction sectors and a substantial increase in investment – has any prospect of reducing this risk.

Too much British capital now flows abroad instead of being invested in Britain. The incentives given the rich to trickle down to the rest in fact trickle abroad to buy foreign property, yachts and investments in the productive capacity of competitors. This enormous outflow is clearly demonstrated in the 2016 leaked bank papers in Panama, Luxembourg and Switzerland. It avoids British taxes and puts up the tax bills for those who remain. Low growth means a zero-sum society in which the gains of wealth leave less for the rest.

Governments have to redress the balances by encouraging the inward flows of money. This pushes up the exchange rate and creates an economy in which everything is for sale. Property markets have to cater for big spenders, not the poor homeless population; regulation has to be kept lax and tax low and avoidable. Indeed, Britain's HMRC has now been permeated by the tax avoidance industry and is deliberately kept so understaffed that it can't cope. Finally, this exposure requires government to run the economy on neoliberal lines to maintain the confidence of foreign Finance. The international financial community is easily frightened and can move its money quickly to somewhere more amenable in the race to the bottom.

Long-term, New Zealand's prospects as an efficient food producer serving expanding Asian and Chinese markets are better than Britain's, which has priced itself out of so many markets and destroyed more of its industrial base than any other country. The threat is to the immediate future of two fragile economies in a world awash with massive money flows. Dependent economies are weaker and less balanced economies face the possibilities of a collapse of confidence in the currency. Britain and New Zealand are more exposed than most because nothing has been done to control the massive money flows. We fly on a wing and a prayer.

CHAPTER TEN

ENDGAME

THE NEOLIBERAL REFORMS IN New Zealand and Britain never produced the promised results. Growth and productivity were both lower than in the glorious post-war decades, unemployment substantially higher. While the rich, particularly the rentiers, benefitted enormously as their money compounded and top pay shot up, the poor, the disabled, the young and those in depressed areas suffered quite disproportionately. People were forced to become more reliant on debt and dangerously high consumer credit as they struggled to survive on stagnating incomes. The ability of Britain and New Zealand to pay their way in the world suffered as manufacturing declined, leading to external deficits and an increase in foreign ownership.

Successive Labour governments at the turn of the 21st century rectified the balances by ending the long underinvestment in health and education, though not housing, but fear of borrowing curtailed their efforts. They failed to increase the top tax rates. Then, in 2009, with Helen Clark's

Labour government in New Zealand voted out and Gordon Brown's in Britain nearing its end, both nations succumbed to the basic weakness of the new economics: the power it gave to unbalanced financial sectors, which were under-regulated, over-funded and freer to pursue their propensity to take ever-bigger risks.

The result was the Great Recession, which started in late 2008 in America with the sub-prime crisis but radiated out to the rest of the world as credit collapsed, banks went bust and loans which should never have been made were called in. At this point policy in Britain and New Zealand, hitherto much the same, diverged.

Britain, with a bigger financial sector, suffered heavily and the incoming Tory government in 2010 seized the opportunity not to revert to the Keynesian policies, but to a new bout of neoliberal medicine, justified by an attack on Labour for overspending and leaving a crisis. This provided the excuse for massive cuts in investment, more tax cuts for the wealthy, more privatisations and cuts in the civil service, reductions in disabled and other benefits, in local government and in all departmental spending except health and education. All this produced a recession from which the country was saved only by the Bank of England's loose monetary policy.

New Zealand was different this time. Less deferential than the British and less likely to rally to calls for the "Dunkirk spirit", its voters had taken their revenge for past punishments and put their politicians on a short leash with proportional representation. They showed their independent spirit again in getting zero-hours contracts – on which a million people work in the UK – banned in New Zealand. Nor did Kiwi ministers have George Osborne's excuse of a crisis. The impact of the Great Recession was far less because the banks had taken fewer risks and were less exposed, and because the country was cushioned by the explosive growth of the new Chinese market.

The New Zealand National government which took office from 2008 talked the neoliberal talk, which had become part of the language and a badge of respectability, but it was no longer driven by that ideology. Instead it pursued more traditional conservative policies which amount to claiming to be fair to all while slipping a couple of aces to the wealthy, and underfunding the economy to keep inflation (and the workers) at bay. So New Zealand got tax cuts for the wealthy, and promises to balance the budget and pay the debt half a decade ahead. Exactly what George Osborne was promising to achieve by more savage methods in Britain.

Neither government could achieve this neoliberal objective. Indeed, it's hardly sensible to do so when recessions require deficit financing as a Keynesian response. With any luck (and the dawn of sense) it's possible that neither will want to because, after nearly four decades of dominating policy in so much of the advanced world, the era of neoliberalism is coming to an end. The European Union remains trapped in austerity by its effort to make an unworkable Euro work for the poorer members. This freezes up the EU, unable to move forward, unwilling to go back.

In Britain, before being thrown out in the turmoil which followed the UK's 2016 referendum vote to "Brexit" from the European Union, an ideologically motivated chancellor struggled to get public spending down. Meanwhile, £4 billion worth of welfare cuts were denied by that collection of radicals the House of Lords, and his follow-up proposal was noisily rejected, leaving him with a hole in his budget. He was unable to take his revenge and fill the gap, because he then lost his job – to a sigh of relief even in his own party.

Neoliberalism is at last on the retreat and not only because it has been seen not to work. Those stern defenders of economic orthodoxy, the IMF and the OECD, have both urged an end to deflation and a commitment to stimulative infrastructure works. There is a growing demand for investment to seize the benefits of interest rates kept artificially low for several years and likely to remain so. Reserve banks are looking to new instruments of monetary management to boost growth, such as quantitative easing (on a massive scale in the Eurozone and Japan), negative interest rates to push commercial banks into more lending and even helicopter money. In New Zealand, the hands of government have been tied by proportional representation and in Australia by the trade unions. In both, populist prime ministers echoed the views of the people, repeating what the polls told them the people want, rather than following any neoliberal prescription. They responded to economic problems by economic tightening, not ideology.

Everywhere there is a growing concern, voiced by such economists as Thomas Piketty, Sir Tony Atkinson and many others, about inequality and its consequences in ever-escalating house prices and increasing poverty. Robert Reich argues that wealth's power and influence must be reduced to save capitalism from itself.

A death knell to the hegemony of neoliberalism was sounded by popular revolt: in New Zealand a referendum installed proportional representation, and two decades later in Britain another voted for Brexit. These peasants' revolts stopped governments imposing neoliberalism on the people as if it were a medicine the nation had to be forced to take for its own good, but they did not bring it to an end as an economic theory; many continue to believe in the power of markets and monetarism, just as some still believe in the second coming or argue that the Earth is flat. Media and politicians still pay lip service to the neoliberal orthodoxies of lower taxes on the wealthy to stimulate investment, on soft-touch regulation and on balanced budgets and zero debt. Yet battle cries which once thrilled and excited business are now less credible and less enthusiastically received than they were in monetarism's golden dawn. This is because their consequences have come through in slower growth, in the slowest recovery from any recession ever, and in an increase in foreign ownership as the long-term failure of both Britain and New Zealand to pay their way in the world creates a need to sell assets to pay for imports they can't otherwise afford.

In both countries, the result of the neoliberal revolution is that everything is for sale, from companies to property and even (in New Zealand) citizenship and legislation, so the commanding heights of the economy, which Labour once threatened to nationalise, are taken over by foreigners, including foreign nationalised competitors. Housing becomes less affordable as the need to raise money opens the housing market to the world and its wealthy, leading in turn to disproportionate prices and centralisation on Auckland and London, where the wealthy prefer to live. As manufacturing shrinks outside London and Auckland both countries become more overbalanced by these two sprawling greedy monsters.

Economies have become lop-sided, because of the triumph of Finance and the need to fund deficits which forced both countries to make themselves attractive to incoming money of all sorts, funny or serious, laundered or dirty. The money poured in to acquire national assets and balance the books. Both set out to attract it by soft regulation, lax enforcement and evadable taxation enforced by undermanned and overstretched public revenue services. Both were effectively turning themselves into tax havens.

This is well short of the glowing prospects held out by Margaret Thatcher and Roger Douglas, all of which have predictably failed to materialise. We're all better off, two nations of greedy consumers, most of us suburb- and city-dwellers rather than proud provincials or denizens of small towns. The disciplines of nation-building are no longer acceptable now that we're all consumers rather than producers. Some are better consumers than others, though most are in debt to pay for their addictions.

Life remains comfortable for a middle class insulated by home ownership, family nest-eggs and professional jobs. Many endure it by what Wolfgang Streeck, in his book *How Will Capitalism End?*, calls "coping, hoping, doping and shopping". He should have added borrowing and debt, the ointment for austerity, but life is less comfortable for the poor, the disabled, the badly educated and those at the bottom of the heap, because the full employment and welfare states created by the post-war settlement have been undermined. Prospects for the young are far gloomier than those which had faced the Baby Boomers after World War II. Jobs are scarcer and less secure in the "gig economy" of agencies, zero-hours contracts and part-time work; debts are greater, incomes flatter, and rocketing house prices impossible to afford. This is no society for the young. It is far more difficult for them to get a foot on the ladder of life, let alone climb it as far as their parents did. As a result, we are no longer one community advancing, improving and benefitting together, but two; the haves, more numerous and more comfortable than in the 1930s, and the have-nots, on whom the pains and penalties of austerity fall disproportionately. Free markets benefit the strong and penalise the weak, who need protection not cuts. They hit the young particularly hard because they find it more difficult to get jobs, impossible to buy houses and are burdened with debt and lower benefits.

The political consequence of neoliberalism has been the creation in Britain of a whole new phenomenon, the left-behind people. They are a tribe whose world has been changed without their consent. They live, mainly, in declining areas hit hard by globalisation and the collapse of old basic industries. They are largely made up of older citizens and blue-collar workers angered by the way their lives have been blighted by the squeeze on their living standards and the flat-lining of their household incomes. In Britain and the US these people have turned not to the radicalism of the Jarrow Marchers of the 1930s but to a largely negative and backward-looking hostility to a system which seems to work against them, and which has scrapped the protection of full employment and imposed a degeneration in their quality of life.

In the US the cry of protest by the people left behind has been Tea Party politics and the surge of populist support for Donald Trump. In Britain, it has emerged in anti-immigrant protests, UKIP voting and the victory of withdrawal from the European Union in the 2016 referendum. In New Zealand, its impact has been less because immigration and the pain of neoliberalism have been less and the decline of whole areas has been paralleled only in the quiet depression of places like Reefton, Wyndham, Lawrence, and other smaller rural centres plus the old timber towns. The result has been not a negative populism of the National Front type, but a drift of population to the cities in New Zealand's more mobile society.

The social balances have been shifted from people and their needs, to wealth and business and their greed. Everything is driven harder to maximise profit, short-term thinking drives out long-term building and business needs prevail over both social requirements and the dictates of nation-building. This imbalance would have been made worse by the arrival of almost total free trade through proposed trade and investment agreements. Both the Pacific and the Atlantic "partnerships" – the Trans Pacific Partnership and the Transatlantic Trade and Investment Partnership – were designed to make the world safer for big multi-nationals to prevail in, but they would have made it more difficult to rebalance lop-sided economies like Britain's and New Zealand's, which have de-industrialised too heavily. The two partnerships did not come to pass because President Trump unilaterally vetoed both, but the difficulties before that had come from the intransigence of the US Congress rather than opposition in or by New Zealand or

Britain. One small benefit may arise for Britain in that, if the European Union is prepared to concede big tariff reductions and market entry for services to the Americans and others, it could be more difficult to refuse them to Britain in the Brexit negotiations.

In this harder, more driven and more basic world, trust, the small civilities, the quality of life and the spirit of public service have suffered most, and we are nastier, meaner and less provident societies. Investment has fallen to record lows as British and New Zealand capital is invested abroad rather than at home. Rising standards of living and faster growth haven't happened as they did before. They should have made life better for the many, not the few, widened opportunities and provided more social facilities and libraries, better social, health and youth services, swimming and sporting facilities. These haven't improved in the way they should have, and are left straining at the seams and starved of resources while company profits escalate. New Zealand author Fiona Farrell, in her book *The Villa at the End of the Empire*, puts it well: "Over the last thirty years the systems that nurtured me have been unpicked quietly and systematically by people with a simple faith in the market as the greatest good. We've laid aside all talk of moral unity, the good and right state of society or collective responsibility for a more bare-knuckled ambition to become a country where it's good to do business."

Given that some businesses cheat, some companies take

short cuts, accounts can be fiddled, tax obligations evaded, markets milked, goods overcharged and short-term profits be preferred to long-term responsibilities, Farrell could have added that a good place to do business can also be a good place for business to "do" the people. It certainly will be unless balance is restored and the countervailing State is once again made powerful and effective enough to fulfil its responsibilities as regulator, defender of the public interest and defender of the people whose protector it should be.

We are at last entering a post-liberal age in which the State is being repaired and the fairy stories which justified the neoliberal revolution are no longer believed. It can't now be seriously argued that lower taxes mean more revenue, that markets are smarter and better than democratic government, that growth comes through cutbacks. Nor can it be said that government borrowing drives out private borrowing, or that money given to the rich will trickle down to the poor, just as the hay fed to horses trickles down to the little sparrows in the road. The age of make-believe is over. Both governments are turning to borrow and spend to revive the economy, rather than obsessing about balancing the budget.

Moreover, after years of being squeezed by austerity and the opening up of markets the people are beginning to refuse to put up with it any longer. The election of President Trump in the US, the Brexit vote in Britain and the rise of extremist parties of the Left and Right in Europe all demonstrate the rising tide of protest and resentment. American figures analysed by the political scientist R.W. Johnson indicate why. In the good years from 1948 to 1973, American productivity rose by 97 percent and real wages by 91 percent. In the neoliberal era from 1973 to 2015 productivity went up 73 percent, but real wages only 11 percent, forcing those lower down the social pyramid, unprotected now by trade unions and job security, to try to keep up by borrowing and having both parents in the workforce. The same trends were apparent, though to a lesser extent, in the rest of the advanced world as economies were tilted against the people who'd been protected by the post-war settlement to the wealthy who'd come to resent it. While this counter-revolution was going on the riches and rewards of those at the top of the heap exploded, political leaders like Bill Clinton and Tony Blair became millionaires, while the people they represented were squeezed. House prices rocketed above the ability of the less well-off to buy, but accommodation for billionaires expanded. The rich flaunted their wealth and lifestyle, the media glamourised it and governments fawned on it. It was a culture of what the French call *la richesse insultante*. No wonder there was an uprising of the unprotected and the people left behind.

It is no wonder also that governments have begun reluctantly to start looking anew for what works. While it is clear that neoliberalism doesn't, no alternative system of economic management has emerged. Austerity lingers on in the Eurozone, imposed now not as a part of a neoliberal reconstruction of the economy, but a consequence of the failure of a monetary union which could never work without a federal political union, rather than separate states. Only in Britain and New Zealand was full-blooded austerity imposed by governments driven by neoliberal ideology and which had the power to do anything they wanted through the elective dictatorship. And only in these two countries was it ended by the people. But while many suggestions are proffered as to its alternative, no one is quite sure what comes next as the age of austerity in the UK and New Zealand comes to an end.

Neoliberalism failed because it was one-sided, and delivered little beyond higher unemployment, slower growth, greater debts, privatised utilities which exploited rather than invested and cuts in government services. Governments weakened the states they had been elected to run, and discounted their roles as protector, investor, stimulator and guide, in favour of giving all power to markets.

A basic mistake. The State has a vital part to play. New Zealand was largely a creation of the State. Even in laissez-faire Britain it had not only determined policy but provided services and utilities, from education of the workforce, to water and power supply, without which the private sector couldn't operate as fairly or effectively. On an authoritative estimate, the British State spends £93 billion on corporate socialism by subsidising, supporting and helping the private sector. This, and the opening up of the State to outsourcing, private Finance and privatisation, have developed a dependency culture in British capitalism and brought it to the point where it is better at leeching on the State than competing in the world.

Indeed, companies can only make profit because they can pass on the environmental and social costs of production to the State, and benefit from the education, health services, roads and protection which the State provides. This is what makes it wrong for companies to dodge their responsibilities by evading and avoiding taxation, which is the social rent they owe.

Only the State can control and regulate powerful multinationals. Only it can protect the people from globalisation and mitigate its effects. In Britain and New Zealand, it failed to do either. Indeed, both welcomed trade and investment partnerships with the US designed to make countries fit for the multinationals to dominate. Neither really succeeded in the essential task of training a skilled workforce to attract industries, retraining those who lost their jobs and supporting areas hard hit by globalisation. Instead, Britain and New Zealand sold off companies, national assets and property to foreigners, then congratulated themselves that this inward flow showed confidence in the country, when it was really taking the returns from grabbing the bargains in a jumble sale triggered to keep the show on the road while driving the exchange rate up to damage the productive economy as they did so.

Britain's problems are deeper and more intractable than those of New Zealand, an efficient food producer in a hungry world. An economy lop-sidedly dependent on Finance has to be shifted back into production to pay its way. Instead of soft regulation to attract foreign capital, Britain needs effective regulation of Finance, foreigners and the utilities to build strong companies, which will need to be helped and encouraged to invest, grow and look to the long term, rather than shareholder value. All this will be a huge task if decline is to be reversed.

Yet in both countries the lesson of experience is not that we need a new economic philosophy or a new ideology, be it socialism, considerate capitalism, new Labour, the corporate state or free or managed trade. Rather, it is that economic policy requires co-operation between the State and the private sector, not the triumph of one over the other.

No doubt a new philosophy will emerge in both Britain and New Zealand. Both Labour parties certainly need one desperately, to replace neoliberalism as it fades into the dustbin of history. It may be called Kindly Capitalism, Considerate Conservatism, Even Newer Labour, Social Democracy, Populism or Corporatism, but attempting to develop this is well beyond the scope of this book. In summing up neoliberalism, the concern must be to learn the lessons of its failure.

They are four. The first is that good economics make for good politics, and bad politics lead to economic failure. Good economics are those which maximise betterment, fairness and growth to improve the lot of the people. Sacrifice that to any ideology – be it Euro-enthusiasm, political prestige or a desire to discipline unions and people – and the results will be bad. Second, the exchange rate is crucial. Success requires a competitive exchange rate and that's one which allows the country to balance its trade in conditions of growth and full employment. Using the exchange rate as a discipline to fight inflation, to weaken the unions or to enrich the rentiers undermines the economy. Thirdly, good economics require balance and co-operation between the State and the private sector, not the triumph of one over the other. Capitalism cheats and the State represses. Markets can energise and provide dynamism. But to make them master is to enthrone inequality and leave the citizens vulnerable. Fourth, a less equal society is a less efficient one. The great rise in inequality makes nations economically less successful. It reduces demand, is prone to more tensions and conflicts and is a less happy place to be. Society is an organism and production a co-operative endeavour. Both are boosted when rewards and growth are fairly and more evenly distributed.

When Tony Blair and John Prescott began to proclaim the virtues of the market and talk of its "rigour" I asked John: "Surely you mean vigour?" "I don't know what the hell Tony means but that's what we've got to say," he replied. Blair was indeed saying rigour and it was then I realised that we were making markets the master not the servant. A dangerous development because the State must regulate markets, run those areas where the market fails and protect those damaged by it. Only the State can do that. And only a society in which the State and private sector work together for the betterment of all can be really successful. We need balance, and an end to economic fairy tales, not a new ideology.

The question is practical. What works for the people. Not for the wealthy, business, multinationals, free trade theory or any sectional or class interest, but the people. All of them, without favouring or giving excessive influence or undue pain to any one section. Fairness and balance are the government's responsibility. Its role must be to ensure that we advance together to build the fairer society which serves the purposes and wellbeing of all.

NOTES

Introduction: A Game of Two Halves

1   John Maynard Keynes: Keynes (1883–1946) was one of the most influential economists of the 20th century and a school of thought bears his name in Keynesian economics. His *General Theory of Employment, Interest and Money* (1936) advocated, among other things, government deficit spending during times of economic downturn to maintain employment.

3   the five "giant evils": Beveridge's report, *Social Insurance and Allied Services*, also known as the Beveridge Report, was published in 1942.

3   Milton Friedman Street: Milton Friedman (1912–2006) was an American economist whose ideas greatly influenced government policies in Britain and New Zealand, and elsewhere, in the late 20th and early 21st centuries. In contrast to Keynsian economics, Friedman's monetarist economics advocated a free market and a restricted role for government in the economy, but proposed that inflation could be controlled through changes in the money supply.

6   Brexit: People in the UK voted 52 percent to 48 percent to leave the European Union in a referendum on 23 June 2016.

Chapter One: The World We Lost

7   Bretton Woods agreement: A United Nations conference in Bretton Woods, New Hampshire, in July 1944, led to both the International Monetary Fund (IMF) and the World Bank and established a system of fixed exchange rates that lasted for nearly 30 years. Under it, all currencies were linked to the US dollar, and the dollar was linked to gold.

7   *"Les Trente Glorieuses"*: The phrase describing a "glorious 30" years, was used by the French economist Jean Fourastié for the title of his book *Les Trente Glorieuses, ou la révolution invisible de 1946 à 1975*, Paris, Fayard, 1979.

7   Friedrich Hayek: Friedrich Hayek (1899–1992) was an Austrian and British economist who was known as a defender of free-market capitalism. He believed that private investment would stimulate growth better than government spending, putting him at odds with John Maynard Keynes.

8   Britain, moving a decade behind New Zealand to a benevolent welfare state: The First Labour Government of New Zealand, which took power in 1935, established the cornerstone of a welfare state with its Social Security Act 1938. By 1941 it had also established free health care. In the UK, the free National Health Service was established by the National Health Service Act 1946.

174

9   "Never had it so good": Conservative leader Harold Macmillan
       uttered the phrase at a rally in Bedford in July 1957, six
       months after becoming Britain's prime minister. Despite being
       sometimes quoted as saying, "You've never had it so good",
       Macmillan told Conservative Party members, "Most of our
       people have never had it so good" because of the prosperity of
       the post-World War II years. "Go around the country, go to
       the industrial towns, go to the farms and you will see a state
       of prosperity such as we have never had in my lifetime – nor
       indeed in the history of this country."

9   A.J.P. Taylor, *English History 1914–1945*, first published by
       Oxford University Press, 1965.

Chapter Two: The Search for New Mates

13   Frank Holmes and the short-lived National Development Council:
       Sir Frank Holmes (1924–2011) was a prominent New Zealand
       economist. An advisor to the government, he led the National
       Development Council, established by a National Party government
       in 1969 but abolished by Labour when it took office in 1972.

13   Michael Shanks, *The Stagnant Society: A Warning*, Penguin
       Books, 1961.

13   Peter Calvocoressi, *World Politics Since 1945*, first published by
       Longman in 1968. The book is regarded as an authoritative
       standard work which has so far gone through nine editions.

14   Correlli Barnett's earlier books are said to have influenced
       members of Margaret Thatcher's cabinet.

14   Anthony Crosland, *The Future of Socialism*, London, Cape, 1956.

17   Reginald Maudling's 1963 "expansion without inflation" budget:
       British Chancellor of the Exchequer Reginald Maudling
       produced a budget which aimed at a 4 percent growth target
       without inflationary consequences in 1963. It achieved its
       growth target perhaps too well – by early 1964, growth exceeded
       6 percent – forcing Maudling the following year to act against
       the resultant inflationary pressures. See Michael J. Stewart,
       *Politics and Economic Policy in the UK Since 1964: The Jekyll and
       Hyde Years*, London, J.M. Dent, 1977.

19   "equal access to a common resource": The Common Fisheries
       Policy of the European Union establishes the rules for
       managing fishing fleets and conserving fish stocks. "Designed
       to manage a common resource, it gives all European fleets equal
       access to EU waters and fishing grounds and allows fishermen
       to compete fairly." See https://ec.europa.eu/fisheries/cfp_en.

19   words later leaked from the Scottish Office: A memo drafted
       by D.K. Rowland of the Scottish fisheries department on
       9 November 1970, leaked and subsequently released under
       the 30-year rule for making information public, said that
       "in the wider context (inshore fisheries) must be regarded as
       expendable". See Christopher Booker and Roland North, *The
       Great Deception: Can the European Union survive?*, Continuum,
       London, 2005.

22   Templeton felt that "the case was coming out strongly for closer
       economic relations": Hugh Templeton, *All Honourable Men:*

Inside the Muldoon cabinet, 1975–1984, Auckland University Press, Auckland, 1995.

Chapter Three: The End of the Golden Weather

The chapter title echoes the title of a play by New Zealander Bruce Mason, *The End of the Golden Weather*, Wellington, Price Milburn, 1962.

26   a three-day work week: British Prime Minister Edward Heath's Three-Day Work Order was designed to limit electricity consumption in response to a generation crisis caused by industrial action by miners. It limited electricity use for commercial users to three days in any given week and was in effect from 1 January to 7 March 1974.

27   Jeremy Thorpe: Liberal Party leader Jeremy Thorpe's political career ended in 1976 when newspaper allegations were made that he had an affair with Norman Scott during the 1960s, when homosexual relationships were illegal in Britain. Thorpe was later acquitted with three others of conspiracy to murder Scott in connection with the incident in which Scott's dog was shot in October 1975. Thorpe died in 2014.

29   Bill Sutch: The economist and senior public servant Dr W.B. Sutch, a household name in New Zealand through his influential books, retired in 1965 after years of suspicion concerning his possible links with the Soviet Union. He was arrested in 1973 after a clandestine night-time meeting in a Wellington park with a known KGB agent stationed at the Soviet embassy, but

was acquitted the following year of passing information to the USSR. He died in 1975.

31 The New Zealand Party: Bob Jones's New Zealand Party, with the slogan "Freedom and Prosperity", was active from 1983 to 1986. It did not win any seats in parliament but is considered to have contributed to the defeat of Robert Muldoon's National Party in 1984 by splitting the Right-wing vote.

31 Jane Kelsey, *The FIRE Economy: New Zealand's Reckoning*, Bridget Williams Books with the New Zealand Law Foundation, Wellington, 2015.

32 Ayn Rand: Ayn Rand was the founder of the American Objectivism movement devoted to individualism and laissez-faire capitalism. Her novels included *The Fountainhead* (1943) and *Atlas Shrugged* (1957). Alan Greenspan, later chairman of the US Federal Reserve, was an early devotee.

32 Sir Keith Joseph, nicknamed the "Mad Monk": See Andrew Denham and Mark Garnett, *Keith Joseph*, Acumen, Chesham, 2001.

33 Roger Douglas, *There's Got to Be a Better Way: A practical ABC to solving New Zealand's major problems*, Fourth Estate Books, Wellington, 1980.

35 Hugh Templeton, *All Honourable Men: Inside the Muldoon cabinet, 1975–1984*, Auckland University Press, Auckland, 1995.

36 The Treasury (New Zealand), *Economic Management: Briefing to the incoming government*, Wellington, 14 July 1984.

37 "Where there is discord,…": Margaret Thatcher quoted the prayer attributed to (but not, in fact, by) St Francis of Assisi

to reporters waiting in Downing St for her return from
Buckingham Palace on becoming prime minister on 4 May
1979. She had previously made notes of what she wanted to
say on a small card, which survives in the Margaret Thatcher
Foundation archive.

40   Geoffrey Palmer, *Unbridled Power? An interpretation of New
Zealand's constitution and government*, Oxford University Press,
1979, reissued without the question mark as *Unbridled Power:
An interpretation of New Zealand's constitution and government*,
Oxford University Press, 1987.

Chapter Four: The Wrecking Gang Arrives

44   a sensible 20 percent devaluation: The defeat of Robert
Muldoon's National Party in New Zealand's snap election in 1984
precipitated a currency crisis because the market believed that the
incoming Labour government would devalue the dollar. In the
period before the new government could be sworn in, Muldoon
ignored the Treasury's advice for devaluation in accordance with
Labour's wishes, relenting only after Labour leader David Lange
went on television to say that Muldoon had put the country "at
risk", and Muldoon's own ministers had threatened to remove
him from his party's leadership. The crisis led to a review of the
Constitution Act, which came into effect in 1986.

44   "economic summit": See Paul C. Dalziel, 'The 1984 economic
summit conference: a search for policy objectives', *New Zealand
Economic Papers*, Vol. 20, Iss. 1, 1986.

45   "She who must be obeyed": The phrase was applied to the all-powerful queen Ayesha in Rider Haggard's story *She: A History of Adventure*, serialised in *The Graphic* magazine in 1886–87 and subsequently published as a book. It was popularised by the 1970s television courtroom drama *Rumpole of the Bailey* when barrister Horace Rumpole used it to refer to his wife, Hilda.

45   "the eyes of Caligula": President Mitterand's description of Thatcher was made by him to one of his ministers and is reported, among other places, in Andrew Marr, *A History of Modern Britain*, Macmillan, 2007.

46   "the lady's not for turning": Thatcher's declaration referenced Christopher Fry's play *The Lady's Not For Burning*, first produced at the Arts Theatre, London, in 1947 and published by the Oxford University Press in 1949.

46   Charles Moore, *Margaret Thatcher: The Authorized Biography, Volume One: Not For Turning*, Allen Lan, London, 2013; *Volume Two: Everything She Wants*, Allen Lane, 2015.

47   Norman Fowler, *A Political Suicide: The Conservatives' voyage into the wilderness*, Politico's, London, 2008.

54   David Lange, *My Life*, Viking, Auckland, 2005.

55   "alibi-ographies": The statement, "All autobiographies are alibi-ographies", suggesting the writers are trying to distance themselves from, or present their own view of, events is attributed to former US congresswoman, diplomat and author Clare Boothe Luce.

58   Mont Pelerin Society: The Mont Pelerin Society, named after

the Swiss resort where it first met in 1947, is an international society devoted to the study and discussion of market-oriented economic systems. An edited version of Roger Douglas's speech to the society in Christchurch on 28 November 1989 can be found on the Centre for Independent Studies (Australia) website at http://www.cis.org.au/app/uploads/2015/04/images/stories/policy-magazine/1990-autumn/1990-6-1-roger-douglas.pdf.

58   Roger Douglas (with Louise Callan), *Unfinished Business*, Random House New Zealand, Auckland, 1993.

61   "You only find who is swimming naked when the tide goes out": This quote, with variations, has been attributed to Warren Buffett repeatedly. It can be found in his Berkshire Hathaway Chairman's Letter for 2001 at http://www.berkshirehathaway.com/2001ar/2001letter.html.

63   with Roger out of the country: An account of Lange's unilateral cancellation of Douglas's tax package in January 1988 can be found in Patrick Massey, *New Zealand: Market liberalisation in a developed economy*, Macmillan, 1995.

63   Whim Wham: The lines quoted are from the poem 'Remedial Politics' by Whim Wham, published in April 1988.

67   Mother of all Budgets: The description that Ruth Richardson applied to her 1991 budget is well remembered. See Te Ara, The Encyclopedia of New Zealand online at http://www.teara.govt.nz/en/photograph/33885/the-mother-of-all-budgets.

67   Ian Cowan, *Not Our Problem*, Mary Egan Publishing, Auckland, 2015.

68   Graham Scott: Peter Roberts, A question of respect. Presidential
      column, ASMS (Association of Salaried Medical Specialists)
      newsletter March 1998, quoted in *Not Our Problem* above.

69   Andrew Dean's interview with Ruth Richardson: See Andrew
      Dean, *Ruth, Roger and Me*, Bridget Williams Books, Wellington,
      2015.

69   Geoffrey Palmer, *Reform: A memoir*, Victoria University Press,
      Wellington, 2013.

70   Alan Gibbs: He was interviewed for the TVNZ series
      'Revolution' produced by Marcia Russell and is quoted in
      her book *Revolution: New Zealand from fortress to free market*,
      Hodder Moa Beckett, Auckland, 1996.

71   "time for a cup of tea": When David Lange put a hold on Roger
      Douglas's single-rate tax package in January 1988, he said it was
      time for the country to pause and have a cup of tea.

Chapter Five: Time For a Break

74   the first general election under proportional representation: New
      Zealand introduced the Mixed Member Proportional system of
      representation (MMP) after a referendum in 1993. Electors cast
      two votes – one for an electorate candidate and one for the preferred
      party of government. Seats in parliament are first filled from the
      elected MPs, and then from "party lists" to ensure that representation
      in the House reflects each party's share of the popular vote.

77   "the longest suicide note in history": This description of the
      Labour Party's 1983 manifesto *New Hope for Britain* was

famously uttered by a former Labour minister, Gerard Kaufman, and is included in the *Oxford Dictionary of Quotations.*

79   Anthony Crosland, *The Future of Socialism*, London, Cape, 1956.

79   the Third Way: The Third Way was a political philosophy that tried to reconcile a centrist path between Right- and Left-wing politics. Sixty years before Blair, the future Conservative prime minister Harold Macmillan advocated a centrist approach in his book *The Middle Way* (Macmillan, London, 1938).

Chapter Six: The Great Recession

89   the "Nixon Shock": Facing a recession, a substantial trade deficit and 6 percent unemployment, US president Richard Nixon in 1971 unveiled an economic reform package which ended the system of fixed exchange rates established at the Bretton Woods conference in 1944.

90   the new Masters of the Universe: The phrase refers to 1980s New York bond traders and investment bankers and was applied to them in Tom Wolfe's novel *Bonfire of the Vanities*, Farrar, Straus, Giroux, New York, 1987.

93   Michael Lewis, *The Big Short: Inside the Doomsday Machine*, Allen Lane, London, 2010.

93   Alistair Darling, on bankers: Alistair Darling, *Back from the Brink: 1000 days at Number 11*, Atlantic, London, 2011.

96   Barry Ritholtz, *Bailout Nation: How greed and easy money corrupted Wall Street and shook the world economy*, Wiley, Hoboken, New Jersey, 2010.

98   G20: G20 describes an international forum of the 20 largest economies and comprises the European Union and Argentina, Australia, Brazil, Canada, China, France, Germany, India, Indonesia, Italy, Japan, South Korea, Mexico, Russia, Saudi Arabia, South Africa, Turkey, the UK and the US.

Chapter Seven: Austerity

101   "You never want a serious crisis to go to waste": Rahm Emanuel's statement was made to a gathering of corporate chief executives at a *Wall Street Journal*-sponsored conference in November 2008, soon after Barack Obama was elected US president. It was reported by Gerald F. Seib in the article 'In Crisis, Opportunity for Obama' in *The Wall Street Journal* on 21 November 2008.

101   A.R.D. Fairburn, *Collected Poems*, Pegasus Press, Christchurch, 1966.

103   Joseph Ward: A version of the anecdote about Joseph Ward mistakenly promising to borrow £70 million instead of £7 million during the 1928 election campaign has been reported by Ward's biographer Dr Michael Bassett on his blog at www.michaelbassett.co.nz/article_ward.htm. "Suffering from diabetes and poor eyesight, Ward inadvertently promised to borrow £70 million in one year to revive New Zealand's economy."

104   Tea Parties: The Tea Party is an American political movement on the Right of the Republican Party.

105   the Washington Consensus: The 10 standard measures recommended by the International Monetary Fund, the World Bank and the US Treasury for countries to recover

from economic crisis were summarised by economist John Williamson in 1989. They were: fiscal policy discipline; redirection of public spending from subsidies to education, health care and investment; tax reform; market-determined interest rates; competitive exchange rates; trade liberalisation; freer foreign direct investment; deregulation; legal security for property rights. See John Williamson (editor), *Latin American Adjustment: How much has happened*, Institute for International Economics, Washington, 1989.

Chapter Eight: The Revenge of the Rich

120   "I'm afraid there is no money": Liam Byrne, chief secretary to the UK Treasury in Gordon Brown's Labour government, left the note to his successor after Labour lost power in 2010. Byrne, the Labour MP for Hodge Hill in Birmingham, later apologised and said that he would regret writing the note "forever" when Conservative leader David Cameron used it against Labour in the 2015 election campaign. See Byrne's article, 'The letter I will regret forever' in *The Guardian*, 9 May 2015.

125   reverse Danegeld: Danegeld was a tax levied on Anglo-Saxon Britons to pay for their defence against, or pay tribute to, Viking invaders in the north and east.

125   Weimar Republic inflation: Between 1921 and 1924, Germany's Weimar Republic suffered devastating hyper-inflation which eventually required it to issue notes denominated in trillions of marks.

131   2013 referendum: A postal ballot was sparked by New Zealand's
       law allowing a citizens-initiated referendum to take place when
       more than 10 percent of registered voters sign a petition asking
       for one. The referendum, held in November and December
       2013, asked voters to indicate their support for the sale of up
       to 49 percent of the state-owned entities Meridian Energy,
       Mighty River Power, Genesis Power, Solid Energy and Air
       New Zealand. The result showed two to one voters were against
       the sale of these state assets. The referendum was not binding,
       Prime Minister John Key said it was an "utter waste of money"
       and the asset sales went ahead.

Chapter Nine: Report on Experience

       The chapter title is also the title of a World War II memoir
       by New Zealand writer and journalist John Mulgan, *Report on
       Experience* (first published posthumously in 1947), Pen & Sword
       Books and Victoria University Press, Wellington, 2010.

135   Danny Dorling, *Inequality and the 1%*, Verso Books, London, 2014.

135   Gini coefficient: The Gini coefficient or Gini index measures a
       country's income distribution. A value of zero expresses perfect
       equality of income; a value of 1 (or 100 percent) represents a
       maximal level of inequality. It was first described in a 1912 book
       in Italian by Corrado Gini. See Lidia Ceriani and Paolo Verme,
       'The Origins of the Gini Index: Extracts from *Variabilità e
       Mutabilità* (1912) by Corrado Gini, *The Journal of Economic
       Inequality*, Vol. 10, Iss. 3, pp 421–443, September 2012.

136 Warren Buffett's tax: Warren Buffett told an NBC television interviewer in 2007 that he should pay more tax, after conducting an informal survey of his office staff. Buffett said he was paying 17.7 percent payroll and income tax, compared with an average of 32.9 percent paid by his employees. "There wasn't anyone in the office, from the receptionist up, who paid as low a tax rate and I have no tax planning; I don't have an accountant or use tax shelters. I just follow what the US Congress tells me to do," he said.

137 Thomas Piketty, *Capitalism in the Twenty-first Century*, Belknap Press, Cambridge, Massachusetts, 2014.

137 Robert Reich, *Saving Capitalism: For the many, not the few*, Alfred A. Knopf, New York, 2015.

144 Hunn Report: A *Report on Department of Maori Affairs*, by J.K. Hunn, deputy chairman of the Public Service Commission and acting secretary for Maori Affairs, was published in 1961. Although a departmental review, it made wider recommendations on social reforms affecting Maori.

144 Ans Westra, *Washday at the Pa*, Caxton Press, 1964. The photographic record of a day in the lives of a rural Maori family caused controversy after the Maori Women's Welfare League complained that the living conditions it portrayed were not typical. The Government Printer which first published the book withdrew its copies and destroyed them, but *Washday at the Pa* was subsequently republished by Caxton Press.

144 Alan Duff, *Once Were Warriors*, Tandem Press, Auckland, 1990.

145 New Zealand's prison population: According to Statistics
     New Zealand, in June 2012, Maori made up 51 percent of
     New Zealand's prison population. See New Zealand's prison
     population at http://www.stats.govt.nz/browse_for_stats/snap-
     shots-of-nz/yearbook/society/crime/corrections.aspx. According
     to the US Department of Justice in 2014, black people made up
     35 to 37 percent of people in custody in the US.

Chapter Ten: Endgame

157 zero-hours contracts: New employment laws passed in New
     Zealand in 2016 gave employees a guaranteed number of hours
     per week and compensation for having to make themselves
     available to work.

161 Wolfgang Streeck, *How Will Capitalism End? Essays on a failing
     system*. Verso Books, London, 2016.

162 the Jarrow Marchers: In 1936, 200 unemployed men marched
     from Jarrow, County Durham, to London with a petition for
     parliament asking for industry to be re-established in their
     town. Parliament received the petition but did not debate it.

163 UKIP: The UK Independence Party is a Right-wing populist
     party in Britain which campaigned for Brexit.

164 Fiona Farrell, *The Villa at the End of the Empire: One hundred
     ways to read a city*, Random House New Zealand Vintage,
     Auckland, 2015.

166 R.W. Johnson: Born in the United Kingdom, resident in
     South Africa, R.W. Johnson is an emeritus fellow at Magdelen

College, Oxford, the author of several books and a South Africa correspondent for *The Sunday Times*.

166   *"la richesse insultante"*: has been translated as extravagant wealth, ostentatiously displayed.

Notes compiled by Ric Stevens.